STRETCHY
LIBRARY LESSONS

Seasons & Celebrations

Pat Miller

Fort Atkinson, Wisconsin

26069

For Bill and Donna Wallace,
my parents, who made so many events a celebration.

Credits:

Pages 67–70: "The Library Dragon" is adapted with permission from *The Library Dragon* by Carmen Agra Deedy. Illustrated by Michael P. White. Peachtree Publishers, 1994.

Pages 74–75: "Spring Vegetables" is adapted with permission from "From Crop to Crunch," by Pat Miller. *LibrarySparks*, May/June 2004.

Pages 85–86: Jokes are used with permission from the named titles in the Read-It! Joke Book series by Michael Dahl. Picture Window Books, 2003.

Published by UpstartBooks
W5527 Highway 106
P.O. Box 800
Fort Atkinson, Wisconsin 53538-0800
1-800-448-4887

Copyright © 2004 by Pat Miller

Contents

Introduction

Each day comes bearing its own gifts. Untie the ribbons.
–Ruth Ann Schabacker

Stretchy Library Lessons: Seasons & Celebrations is for those times when you want to celebrate in the library with your students. Like any celebration, these include fun with games, puzzles, contests, drama and even some songs. And what would a celebration be without gifts? This book includes several gifts for you in the form of ideas that can be made tangible and implemented across the curriculum for numerous activities.

This book is slightly different from its predecessors. In the four previous Stretchy Library Lessons books, the lessons were designed to give librarians ideas for adapting lessons to fit a 20-minute time frame. An additional lesson extended the activities to fill a 45-minute teaching block. In *Seasons & Celebrations*, book five, there are still ten 20-minute lessons, but a variety of extension ideas, rather than just one, are also included

The celebrations are curriculum related and many are close to the interests of children. Whether you are looking for a special way to celebrate student birthdays (and increase your collection) or to capitalize on children's love of dogs, these lessons can help you. They provide a getaway for each month. Select several lessons each year to promote learning, but also add some fun and zest for both you and your students.

How to Use This Book

Stretchy Library Lessons: Seasons & Celebrations has 10 lessons that can be extended by a variety of additional ideas. Read them over and select those that appeal to your sense of fun, your curriculum and your students' needs. All of the lessons are designed to appeal to multiple intelligences, learning styles and reading abilities. The activity index on page 8 lets you know which activities are available for each celebration. Many of the activities can be used throughout the year, in conjunction with the seasonal activity or by themselves.

Each Stretchy Library Lesson includes:

- **A Quotation to Introduce the Theme.** Use it on a bookmark with clip art if desired.

- **A Range of Grades.** The lessons are K–5, though they can be adapted for preschoolers, special needs students and sixth graders.

- **A Purpose.** There may be more than one to help library media specialists integrate the lessons with class curriculum, district and state media literacy standards and social and emotional goals.

- **The Format.** Listing the format (game, contest, read-aloud, etc.) helps you appeal to different learning styles.

- **A List of Materials.** These are readily available or easily made and should be gathered before you teach the lesson.

- **Items to Prepare in Advance.** If you teach all grades each day as I do, your lesson materials need to be well organized because there is little time between classes. This section tells you what needs to be made, purchased or found before a class comes in.

- **Activity Directions.** Most of the main activities can be taught in 20 minutes. The activities include all forms, worksheets and patterns that you will need.

- **Resources.** Lots of books are listed with annotations to share in storytime or recommend to students. Rather arbitrary grade levels have been assigned. Special effort was made to include fiction and nonfiction that can be paired, multicultural stories and good books for a range of ages. The resource books can be used instead of the featured title or as an extension. I tried to include newer works, all of which were in print or available from bookstores or online as I wrote this. Always put these or similar books on display near your teaching area in case a teacher or child wants to extend their learning. The Web sites are current as of this printing, but if you get an error message, perform a keyword search on the Web site title. Be sure the title is enclosed in quotation marks.

Additional Activities

Extend the learning if your class time is longer, or to additional class times if the theme continues to interest students and/or fit with your curriculum. The activities are meant to be selected in any order and do not depend on the main activity or one another.

 Gifts. There are five gifts for you. They are my recipes for things like a Birthday Bear tradition or a shadow stage. I've made and used all five for years and taught others to make them. Once made, these items can be used through the years.

 Math Activities. Math is rarely integrated into library lessons. There are three math activities in this book. In the Pet Month activities, a writing activity has been included instead of a mathematical one.

 Songs/Poems. Capitalize on your students' musical intelligence and add to the fun by using songs, poems and chants with lessons. You will find five of them in this book.

 Drama Activities. I have used Reader's Theater with students from first through fifth grade and the reaction is always the same, "Can we do it again?" There are links to eight drama activities, as well as the full script and character signs for *The Library Dragon*.

 Games. There are eight curriculum related games in this book. Construct them once and use them for dozens of classes over the upcoming years. Your students will love you for playing with them.

 Logic Puzzles. Higher-level thinking is important and is best taught through application. Duplicate the six puzzles and use them with or without the themes. Older students will enjoy constructing their own.

 Contests. The four contests I've designed can be modified and used with grades K–5. For prizes, offer library passes, coupons for an extra book at checkout, free books, bookmarks, pencils or other items. It may be enough for students to have their names announced in the morning and/or posted on the library wall.

Computer Activities. The seven computer activities I've included can be used within the lessons or introduced and used independently in the following week(s). If they are to be used independently, post instructions at each computer station.

The book concludes with a bibliography of all the books and Web sites mentioned in the activities. Duplicate the pages if desired, highlight the needed titles and send the list to your book vendors that offer a typing service.

Wishing you the very best as you find big and small things to celebrate in your library.

Yesterday's the past and tomorrow's the future.
Today is a gift—which is why they call it the present.
–Bil Keane

Activity Index

Months & Celebrations	Grade Level	Math/Writing Activities	Songs/Poems/Chants	Drama Activities	Games	Logic Puzzles	Contests	Computer Activities	Gifts
August Birthdays	K–5	X	X	X	X	X		X	X
September Autumn	K–5			X	X			X	X
October Hobby Month	K–3	X				X			
November Teddy Bear Day	K–5		X	X	X		X		X
December Winter	3–5			X	X	X		X	
January Celebrating Firsts	K–5			X	X	X	X	X	
February Library Lovers Month	2–5		X		X	X	X		
March Spring	K–3	X		X	X			X	
April Humor Month	3–5		X	X	X			X	X
May Pets Month (2 lessons)	K–2 3–5	X	X	X		X	X	X	X

Birthdays

Birthdays are good for you. Statistics show that the people who have the most live the longest.

–Reverend Larry Lorenzoni

Mascot Birthday

Grades: K–5

Purposes:

- To make individuals feel special on their birthday.

- To celebrate the universality of celebrating one's birth day.

Format: Read Aloud, Birthday Celebration

Materials:

- selected books

- party decorations

- party favors *(optional)*

- fake birthday cake (Party stores carry a honeycomb version. I made mine by gluing two circles of Styrofoam to an inexpensive plastic birthday plate. I used tacky glue to adhere quilt batting to the edges and the top. It looks very much like white frosting. Then I glued on sugar letters to spell "Happy Birthday Kippy Joe" [our mascot]. I made a dent in the center of the cake and glued in a numeral candle.)

Prepare in Advance: Display the books and put up the decorations. Make or purchase the cake and set it up. You might want to supply party favors, like small bags of M&M's® or a sandwich bag with Teddy Grahams®. If so, gather those.

Activity Directions:

1. For younger grades, we celebrate Kippy Joe's birthday. He is our Folkmanis® bear puppet mascot. If you don't have a mascot, perhaps you could celebrate the birthday of a favorite character or author.

2. Share your favorite birthday books or use one of the books on pages 13–14.

3. Give each student a birthday bookmark or party favor. To celebrate, allow them to check out an additional birthday book. A fun activity is to ask students to pair up and choose the extra book as a "gift" for their partner. The partner would check out the gift book.

4. For older grades, share birthday customs from around the world and invite them to tell about theirs.

5. Allow older students to also check out an additional book, allowing partner "gifts" if desired.

 # The Birthday Bear

Make a fuss over your students on their birthday and build your collection at the same time.

Materials:

- a large birthday bulletin board decorator (available at teacher supply stores) that has a shape for each month's birthday

- a small bear that will sit, especially if it says "Happy Birthday" on its chest or sweater

- a birthday bear announcement form (see page 15)

- an apron that says "A book is a present you can open again and again" (Make one by purchasing a blank apron at a craft store. Write the message with colored markers or squeeze paint, or use computer clip art and fonts to print it on iron-on transfer paper.)

- plastic book bags that say "Good Books are Good Friends" from Upstart (Item #39047, 25 bags per package, **www.highsmith.com**)

- bookmarks that say, "Good Books are Good Friends" and Happy Birthday to _____, (date) _____. (Make them by laminating colored paper, affixing the Good Book sticker [available from Upstart, 200 per pkg. #44865] to the top and writing the information with a fine tip black permanent marker.)

- birthday bookplates (KidStamps has the one we use. Order at **www.kidstamps.com.** It says, "This book is given in honor of the ___th birthday of _____. Date: ____." There is a picture of a fat cat wearing a party hat and holding a balloon.)

Activity Directions:

1. When a child has a birthday, they have the much-publicized option of having the birthday bear visit. I'm the birthday bear, and I arrive in the child's classroom on his or her birthday, wearing my apron and carrying the birthday book in a special bag. For $15, the child can select any book in the library.

2. Put the bookplate in the front and check the book out to the child. Then write his or her name on the birthday board. Ours is in our library hallway.

3. On the birthday, have the principal read the birthday announcement. Then the birthday bear goes to the class to read the book aloud. If it is a chapter book, read the summary and 10 minutes of the book. The child gets to keep the waterproof book bag and the bookmark. The stuffed birthday bear sits on the child's desk all day (optional for fourth and fifth grade), and the book goes home to be shared with the family and then returned to the library to be kept as a remembrance and shared with the school.

4. Stress that the book is a gift from the birthday child to his class and school. And of course, the book is the only gift that can be opened again and again. (Though one of my first graders said a nice car is also a gift that can be opened again and again.)

 # Birthday Bar Graph

Give each student a die-cut birthday cake that is color-coded by grade. Have the students write their name and day of birth on the cake. Then have them add their cakes to a large birth month bar graph bulletin board in each grade level hall or in the library. Use the tags on page 16 as the base for each bar.

 # "Monday's Child"

"Monday's Child"

Monday's child is fair of face,
Tuesday's child is full of grace,
Wednesday's child is full of woe,*
Thursday's child has far to go,
Friday's child is loving and giving,
Saturday's child works hard for its living,
But the child that's born on the Sabbath day,
Is bonny and blithe and good and gay.
   Traditional

(*I change this line to read "Wednesday's child has much to know.")

Enlarge the traditional rhyme on a chart tablet and have the children say it with you. Children will most likely not know whether they are a Monday or a Tuesday child, so have a calendar of their birth years handy. Find calendars at the 10,000 Year Calendar Web site **www.calendarhome.com/tyc.** Simply type in the year and click "Year at a Glance."

As students tell you their birthdays, tell them their day and have them sit in seven groups. Make a bar graph to show the distribution of birthdays by using the Birthday Graph transparency on page 17. Put an "X" in each box to represent one child. To make the transparency reusable without having to wash it, place Unifix cubes, buttons or pennies in the boxes to indicate that the square is filled.

Then ask students the following questions:

- On which day were the most children born? The least?

- If we put the days in order from the one with the greatest number of children to the least, how would we number them? (Use a transparency pen to number the columns in order at the top.)

- For older children, ask them to do some simple addition and subtraction by asking questions like "How many children were born on Tuesday and Thursday together?" Subtraction questions could be "How many fewer children were born on Saturday than on Friday?"

 *Moira's Birthday*

Moira's Birthday *Reader's Theater Script*

www.qesn.meq.gouv.qc.ca/schools/bchs/rtheatre/sample.htm

Students will enjoy acting out Canadian Robert Munsch's book, *Moira's Birthday* (Annick Press, 1988). A teacher at Baie Comeau High School in Quebec, Canada wrote the script. There are parts for eight readers. You can add two more parts by labeling the narrator parts as narrator #1, #2 and #3.

 **Birthday Lotto**

To play:

Give each student a birthday lotto card and a sandwich bag with lima beans, buttons or Smartees®. Show a transparent version of each picture on the overhead projector. Students study the picture, and then search their card to find the match. Be sure they cover the square that says "Happy Birthday!" as a free space before beginning play.

To make the game:

1. Make 25 copies of the grid on page 19. Glue them to construction paper that is slightly larger. Make a transparent copy of all pictures from page 18 (enlarge if desired).

2. Make 20 copies (not 25) of the picture page and cut the pictures apart. Set the pictures in piles and lay out the 25 grids.

3. Pick up the pile of Happy Birthday! squares. This is the free space. Lay the picture on the first square, first column of the first card. On the second card, put it in the first square, second column, and then the first square, third column of the third card. Proceed square by square until all 25 cards have a free space. Then pick up the pile of cake pictures. Begin with the second square of the second column on the first card. When you use up that pile of pictures, select the next pile and continue. There are more pictures than squares to help make the cards different.

4. Finally, use a glue stick to adhere the pictures. Since you will be laminating the cards, use only enough glue to keep the picture in place before laminating. Allow 24 hours drying time, then laminate the game cards.

Birthday Gifts

Duplicate a class set of the logic puzzle from page 20. Using the clues, have students place an "X" in the box when they determine that a person would not have given the gift. Place a star if that is the correct gift. Once a star is determined, remember to "X" all of the other boxes in the star's row and column.

For a more kinesthetic experience that saves paper and toner, mount a class set of logic puzzles on construction paper and laminate. Give each student a sandwich bag with black and white beans. Have them use the black beans as the "yes" markers and the white as "no" markers. After you share the answers, students return the beans to their bag and the set is ready for the next class.

Answers:

Eric	book
Van	race car
Carolyn	Rollerblades
Bonnie	video game
Royce	teddy bear

Plan a Party

Zoom Party

pbskids.org/zoom/party

Have students use this site to plan their own birthday party. It includes 34 recipes for snacks and sweets like mini tacos and banana smunchies as well as simple main dishes. There are also recipes for drinks and seven fun cakes including one baked in ice cream cones. For an outdoor party, there are instructions for 17 outdoor games like Balloon Pop Relay and Avoid the Octopus. Finally, students can choose a creative activity for themselves and their friends as a party favor all can make and take home. Some ideas include Button Bracelets and Popsicle Stick Puzzles.

Resources

Books:

Birthdays Around the World by Mary Lankford. William Morrow & Co., 2000. (K–5) Customs and ideas come from Finland, Malaysia, Mexico, New Zealand, Philippines, Netherlands and Sweden.

Birthdays Around the World series by Cheryl L. Enderlein. Capstone Press, 1998. (2–5) This series gives background facts about the people and country, and shows the customs involved in gift giving, food and activities on a birthday. Books include a glossary, index and suggestions for books, Internet sites and addresses to write for more information. There are also instructions for making a birthday food or craft. Titles include *Celebrating Birthdays in Australia, Celebrating Birthdays in Brazil, Celebrating Birthdays in China* and *Celebrating Birthdays in Russia.*

Celebrating a Quinceañera: A Latina's Fifteenth Birthday Celebration by Diane Hoyt-Goldsmith. Holiday House, 2002. (3–5) In the Mexican-American culture, the quinceañera is the time for the extended family to celebrate a young woman's transition from childhood to adulthood. Includes detailed color photographs of a Mexican-American family as they celebrate together. This would be a good book to read aloud and have students look for similarities and differences in how families celebrate birthdays.

¡Fiesta! by Ginger Foglesong Guy. Greenwillow Books, 1996. (K–2) This is a counting book that follows the pattern: "Una canasta / One basket…¿Qué más? / What else?" until the book ends with children, a piñata and a fiesta.

Happy Birthday Everywhere by Aileen Erlbach. Millbrook Press, 1997. (K–5) Find greetings and customs from 19 countries with recipes for food, directions for games and crafts and music and words for nine versions of "Happy Birthday to You."

Hooray, A Piñata! by Elisa Kleven. Dutton, 1996. (K–3) Clara befriends her dog piñata and becomes so attached to it that she can't bear to break it on her birthday. Her friend Samson gifts her with the perfect solution. (Author's note explains that the piñata began in Italy as a pignatte and traveled to Mexico via Spain.)

Moira's Birthday by Robert Munsch. Annick Press, 1988. (K–2) Moira thinks nothing of inviting her class to her birthday and ordering 250 pizzas. Guaranteed to get younger students laughing.

Not Yet, Yvette by Helen Ketteman. Albert Whitman, 1992. (K–2) Yvette is so excited about helping her father prepare for her mother's birthday that she can't help but ask if it's time for the birthday every few minutes!

A Picnic in October by Eve Bunting. Harcourt, 1999. (K–3) Tony thinks it's dumb to have a picnic on Ellis Island for Grandma's birthday. Grandma wants to relive where she saw Lady Liberty for the first time as a child. But Tony meets an immigrant family on the island and comes to understand Grandma's love for the Lady with the Lamp.

Yoko's Paper Cranes by Rosemary Wells. Hyperion, 2001. (K–5) Yoko the kitten misses her grandmother in Japan so she makes origami cranes for Grandmother's birthday.

Web sites:

KidStamps
www.kidstamps.com

Moira's Birthday *Reader's Theater Script*
www.qesn.meq.gouv.qc.ca/schools/bchs/rtheatre/sample.htm

10,000 Year Calendar
www.calendarhome.com/tyc

Upstart
www.highsmith.com

Zoom Party
pbskids.org/zoom/party

Birthday Bear Announcement

Birthday: _____   Announce on: _____

The Birthday Bear will be coming to
M _____'s class to
celebrate the _____th birthday of
_____

She has donated a book to the library
in honor of her special day.

Thank you, _____.

We hope you have a very happy birthday!

Birthday: _____   Announce on: _____

The Birthday Bear will be coming to
M _____'s class to
celebrate the _____th birthday of
_____

He has donated a book to the library
in honor of his special day.

Thank you, _____.

We hope you have a very happy birthday!

Birthday Bar Graph Month Tags

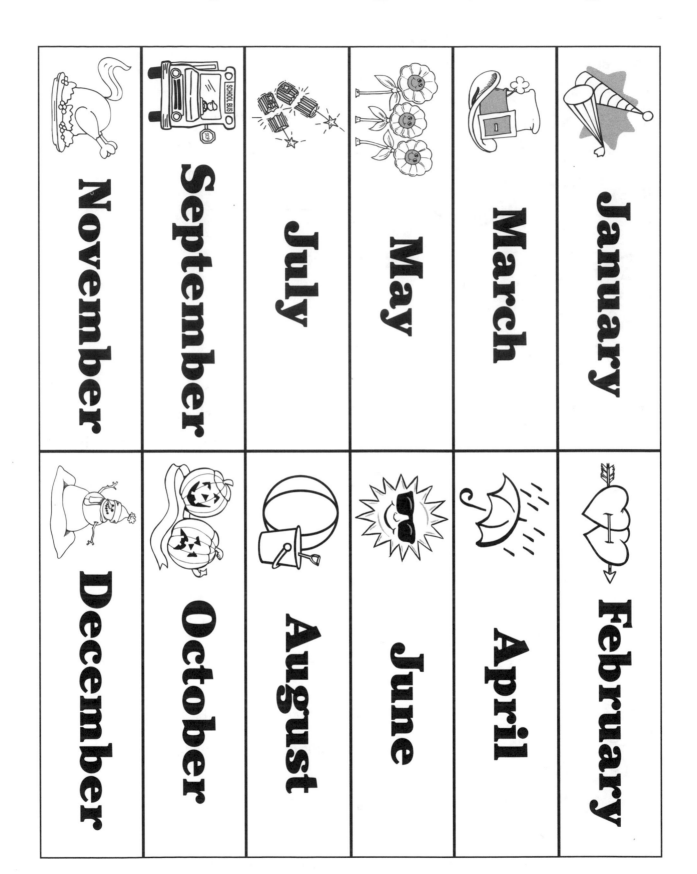

Birthday Graph

Sunday	Monday	Tuesday	Wednesday	Thursday	Friday	Saturday

Birthday Lotto Pictures

Birthday Lotto Card

Birthday Lotto

Birthday Logic Puzzle

Can you match each child to his or her gift? Place an "X" in the box when you determine that a person would not have given the gift. Place a star in the box for the correct gift. Once a star is determined, remember to "X" all of the boxes in the star's row and column.

	Video Game	Book	Teddy Bear	Race Car	Rollerblades
Eric					
Van					
Carolyn					
Bonnie					
Royce					

Clues

1. Bonnie and Royce's gifts do not have wheels.

2. Carolyn's gift will help her get exercise.

3. Bonnie's gift plugs in.

4. Eric's gift can be opened again ... and again.

Autumn

Autumn's the mellow time.
–William Allingham

Leaves Are Falling  MAIN ACTIVITY

Grades: K–5 (Depends on the difficulty of the books shared.)

Purpose:

- To understand why leaves appear to change color and the climactic conditions that cause the change.

Format: Read Aloud, Video on Computer, Game on the Internet

Materials:

- *Autumn Leaves* by Ken Robbins (Scholastic, 1998)

- *Autumn Leaves* by Gail Saunders-Smith (Capstone Press, 1998)

- *Fall Leaves Fall!* by Zoe Hall (Scholastic, 2000)

- *How Leaves Change* by Sylvia Johnson (Lerner Publishing, 1986)

- color leaf identification sheets for each student or pair from Common Fall Leaves at **www.conservation.state.mo.us/nathis/seasons/fall/fleaves/fleaves.htm**

- computers for students and/or display computer with projector device

- leaf identification books and real leaves on display *(optional)*

Prepare in Advance: Make color copies of the leaf identification chart on the Web site for each player or pair of players and laminate on construction paper. Mount the Autumn Leaves and Leaf Invaders Web sites listed on page 24 on your display computer and set up the projector, or place the sites in the favorites folder for independent use on each library computer. Select a book for each grade level.

Optional: Collect leaves from your area. Mount them on foam board with the name of the leaf below each. Display leaf identification books from your collection.

Activity Directions:

1. Read aloud one of the selected books, or view the video at the Autumn Leaves Web site. Then run the quiz on the same site to check students' knowledge of how leaves appear to change color in the autumn.

2. Distribute the leaf identification sheet. Have students carefully study the shapes and colors of the leaves. Point out which leaves are found in your area.

3. Demonstrate the "Leaf Invaders" game to students. Using their identification skills, they name the falling leaf. If they are correct, they earn points. Leaves fall faster as students identify more, adding to the excitement and challenge. They won't see falling leaves the same again!

 # Quickie Tic-Tac-Toe

Materials:

- 4 thick pieces of yarn

- 5 copies on card stock of the X's and O's from page 25

- water-based marker or chalk

- clear tape

- transparency of page 26

Directions:

1. Tape the yarn to a door, window or other smooth surface. The pieces of yarn should form a tic-tac-toe grid. Be sure squares formed are large enough to place the 4" X's and O's inside. An alternate version is to use the 2" shapes on the overhead transparency.

2. Cut numbers from the transparency and adhere them to the center of each square on the smooth surface.

3. Attach a small piece of tape to each X or O to attach to the surface as you play.

4. When a child answers a question correctly, he or she names the number of the square where the figure should go.

5. The first team to form tic-tac-toe is the winner. The winner might also be the team that wins the most games in a set time limit.

 # School Stories

Three Sideways Stories From Wayside School *Reader's Theater Script*
www.aaronshep.com/rt/RTE32.html
Share some humor as the school year begins with these three stories by Louis Sachar. They are for nine readers. You may wish to assign different sets of readers for each story.

Wemberly Worried *Reader's Theater Script*
www.readinglady.com/Readers_Theater/Scripts/wemberly.doc
For younger students, act out *Wemberly Worried* by Kevin Henkes. Wemberly worries about everything before the first day of school, and has a hard time enjoying herself because of her fears. Ten readers can participate with the script.

 # Seasonal Tic-Tac-Toe

Copy pages 29–30. Divide the class into two teams (X's and O's) and ask each team to name the season from an event you read from pages 27–28. Teams earn an X or an O for each correct answer. Or you may want to use pages 27–28 as worksheets.

 # Leaf Catching

Students can practice hand-eye coordination as well as their mouse skills with these games.

Fall Fever
www.funschool.com/php/games/game.php?g=arcade_1d2_ds1
An elf holding a basket is at the bottom of the screen. Students use the arrow keys to move him side to side to catch leaves, which fall faster as they catch more of them.

Fall Online Games
www.kidsdomain.com/games/fall.html
In "Fun in the Garden," sort the fruits and vegetables. Find ten differences between pictures of squirrels or scarecrows, and play "Thanksgiving Feast" by catching healthy foods and avoiding junk food.

 # Resources

Books:

Animals in the Fall by Gail Saunders-Smith. Capstone Press, 1997. (K–2)

Autumn by Terri DeGezelle. Capstone Press, 2002. (K–2)

Autumn: An Alphabet Acrostic by Steven Schnur. Clarion Books, 1997. (2–5) Acrostic poetry that captures the sights, sounds and smells of autumn.

Autumn Leaves by Ken Robbins. Scholastic, 1998. (K–3)

Autumn Leaves by Gail Saunders-Smith. Capstone Press, 1998. (K–2)

Autumn: Signs of the Season Around North America by Mary Pat Finnegan. Picture Window Books, 2002. (2–3)

A Cold Day by Lola M. Schaefer. Capstone Press, 1999. (K–2)

Fall by Darlene Stille. Compass Point Books, 2001. (2–3)

Fall Harvest by Gail Saunders-Smith. Capstone Press, 1998. (K–2)

Fall Leaves Fall! by Zoe Hall. Scholastic, 2000. (K–1)

How Leaves Change by Sylvia Johnson. Lerner Publishing, 1986. (K–2)

In November by Cynthia Rylant. Harcourt, 2000. (2–3)

Last Leaf First Snowflake to Fall by Leo Yerxa. Orchard Books, 1994. (2–4)

The Nature and Science of Autumn by Jane Burton and Kim Taylor. Gareth Stevens, 1999. (3–5)

One Fall Day by Molly Bang. Greenwillow Books, 1994. (K–2)

Seasons by Lisa Trumbauer. Capstone Press, 2000. (K–2)

Sideways Stories from Wayside School by Louis Sachar. William Morrow & Co., 1998. (3–5)

Wemberly Worried by Kevin Henkes. Greenwillow Books, 2000. (K–2)

Web sites:

Autumn Leaves
www.brainpop.com/science/ecology/autumnleaves/index.weml?&tried_cookie=true

Common Fall Leaves
www.conservation.state.mo.us/nathis/seasons/fall/fleaves/fleaves.htm

Fall Crafts
www.enchantedlearning.com/crafts/fall
Includes simple crafts, bulletin board ideas, shape books, fall stories and much more.

Fall Fever
www.funschool.com/php/games/game.php?g=arcade_ld2_ds1

Fall Online Games
www.kidsdomain.com/games/fall.html

Leaf Invaders
www.conservation.state.mo.us/nathis/seasons/fall/swleaf/swleaf.htm

Science U: Seasons Reasons
www.scienceu.com/observatory/articles/seasons/seasons.html
Older students can read about why we have seasons and see a sped-up Earth making its rotation on its axis to produce the different seasons.

Three Sideways Stories From Wayside School *Reader's Theater Script*
www.aaronshep.com/rt/RTE32.html

Wemberly Worried *Reader's Theater Script*
www.readinglady.com/Readers_Theater/Scripts/wemberly.doc

Tic-Tac-Toe Symbols

Tic-Tac-Toe Grid

1	2	3
4	5	6
7	8	9

Seasonal Tic-Tac-Toe

Activity	Season
Folks wear a heavy coat, hat and gloves.	
You'll need your umbrella because it rains a lot.	
Long hot days help crops and gardens grow.	
It's time to harvest apples and pumpkins.	
It's fun to play in the snow.	
Birds begin to fly south.	
Flowers bud and then bloom for the first time in months.	
Squirrels gather nuts for the cold weather ahead.	
Trees shed their leaves.	
Animals who have hibernated come out into the sun.	
Droughts occur most often in this season.	
Many baby animals are born in this season.	
The most popular season for swimming.	
Some rabbit's fur changes from brown to white.	
People ride on sleds or in sleighs.	
Blizzards can occur in this season.	
Holidays like Halloween and Thanksgiving happen in this season.	
Bears, frogs and groundhogs hibernate.	
Hurricanes are most common in this season.	
This season begins on June 21 or 22.	

Seasonal Tic-Tac-Toe (continued)

Activity	Season
In this season, we celebrate many holidays, including Christmas, New Year's Day and Valentine's Day.	
Trees stop making food for themselves.	
The season when students don't go to school much.	
Animals have to work hard to find food in this season.	
This is the season when nature seems to rest.	
When the Northern Hemisphere is having winter, the Southern Hemisphere is having this season.	
In this season, the days keep getting shorter.	
Bears gain a lot of weight this season to prepare for the next season.	
This season begins on December 21 or 22.	
The season in which we celebrate Easter, Cinco de Mayo and Mother's Day.	
People enjoy fishing through holes in the ice.	
Snow melts to water the farmer's crops.	
The season that contains Father's Day, the Fourth of July and Labor Day.	
Monarch butterflies fly up to 3,000 miles during this season.	
This season begins on March 19, 20 or 21.	
This season begins in the Northern Hemisphere when Earth's axis points away from the sun.	
This is the season of the harvest moon when the moon is so bright that farmers can work at night.	
In this season, the daylight lasts longer each day.	
This season begins on September 22 or 23.	
Off the coast of California, humpback and blue whales begin to migrate to warmer waters.	

Seasonal Tic-Tac-Toe Answers

Activity	Season
Folks wear a heavy coat, hat and gloves.	**Winter**
You'll need your umbrella because it rains a lot.	**Spring**
Long hot days help crops and gardens grow.	**Summer**
It's time to harvest apples and pumpkins.	**Autumn**
It's fun to play in the snow.	**Winter**
Birds begin to fly south.	**Autumn**
Flowers bud and then bloom for the first time in months.	**Spring**
Squirrels gather nuts for the cold weather ahead.	**Autumn**
Trees shed their leaves.	**Autumn**
Animals who have hibernated come out into the sun.	**Spring**
Droughts occur most often in this season.	**Summer**
Many baby animals are born in this season.	**Spring**
The most popular season for swimming.	**Summer**
Some rabbit's fur changes from brown to white.	**Winter**
People ride on sleds or in sleighs.	**Winter**
Blizzards can occur in this season.	**Winter**
Holidays like Halloween and Thanksgiving happen in this season.	**Autumn**
Bears, frogs and groundhogs hibernate.	**Winter**
Hurricanes are most common in this season.	**Summer**
This season begins on June 21 or 22.	**Summer**

Seasonal Tic-Tac-Toe Answers (continued)

Activity	Season
In this season, we celebrate many holidays, including Christmas, New Year's Day and Valentine's Day.	Winter
Trees stop making food for themselves.	Winter
The season when students don't go to school much.	Summer
Animals have to work hard to find food in this season.	Winter
This is the season when nature seems to rest.	Winter
When the Northern Hemisphere is having winter, the Southern Hemisphere is having this season.	Summer
In this season, the days keep getting shorter.	Autumn
Bears gain a lot of weight this season to prepare for the next season.	Autumn
This season begins on December 21 or 22.	Winter
The season in which we celebrate Easter, Cinco de Mayo and Mother's Day.	Spring
People enjoy fishing through holes in the ice.	Winter
Snow melts to water the farmer's crops.	Spring
The season that contains Father's Day, the Fourth of July and Labor Day.	Summer
Monarch butterflies fly up to 3,000 miles during this season.	Autumn
This season begins on March 19, 20 or 21.	Spring
This season begins in the Northern Hemisphere when Earth's axis points away from the sun.	Winter
This is the season of the harvest moon when the moon is so bright that farmers can work at night.	Autumn
In this season, the daylight lasts longer each day.	Spring
This season begins on September 22 or 23.	Autumn
Off the coast of California, humpback and blue whales begin to migrate to warmer waters.	Autumn

Hobby Month

Many men go fishing all of their lives without knowing that it is not fish they are after.
–Henry David Thoreau

Rock Collecting

 MAIN ACTIVITY

Grades: K–3

Purpose:

- To share information about hobbies.

Format: Book Sharing, Souvenir, Writing Exercise

Materials:

- *Sylvester and the Magic Pebble* by William Steig (Simon & Schuster, 1988)

- cloth bag containing about 30 smooth river stones (available at hobby or craft stores)

- cause-and-effect strips from page 32

- magnetic board

- magnetic tape

- green and pink paper

- 6" plush Sylvester (available at **www.babyant.com/bt037114.html**)

- collection of labeled rocks

- books listed on pages 34–35

- classroom activity-writing materials *(optional)*

Prepare in Advance: Locate or make a cloth bag. Purchase river stones. Put about 30 of them into the cloth bag before each class. Write causes on green sentence strips and effects on pink sentence strips. Attach a small piece of magnetic tape to the back of each. Locate a collection of labeled rocks. Get book and plush character.

Activity Directions:

1. Read *Sylvester and the Magic Pebble* aloud.

2. Review the story events with the students. If you have the plush Sylvester, after he wishes on the red pebble, unzip the zipper on his spine, pull out the purple "rock" and cover him with it. The pebble is on the outside of the rock now.

3. Distribute the cause-and-effect strips. Ask the student with number 1 to place it on the magnetic board. Then the student with the effect comes up. Before he or she does, ask students what they think the effect would be.

4. Show students the labeled rock collection and talk about where rocks for a collection can be found. Do any of your students have a rock collection?

5. Talk about collections. Share one of the books on collections listed on pages 33–35. Ask students what they collect. (*Optional:* Allow students to bring their collections to the library to display or share with the class.)

6. Allow each student to reach into the cloth bag (no peeking!) and pull out his or her own magic pebble.

7. If desired, when students return to class, they can write an adventure about how they found their magic pebble and what they wished for with it.

Causes	Effects
1. Sylvester searches for rocks for his collection.	He finds a red, shiny pebble.
2. Sylvester wishes the rain would stop.	It stops in midair.
3. Sylvester sees a lion.	He is frightened.
4. Sylvester is frightened.	He wishes he is a rock.
5. Sylvester doesn't come home.	His parents worry.
6. Sylvester's parents are worried.	They look around the neighborhood for him.
7. Sylvester is lost.	His parents go to the police.
8. Sylvester is gone for a year.	His parents go to a picnic to relieve their sadness.
9. Sylvester's parents find a pebble.	Sylvester's mother wishes he could see it.
10. Sylvester magically appears.	Everybody is happy.

 # Charting Collections

As an extension activity in the library or classroom, share the four collection books listed below and have students complete the chart on page 36. You can also use the last row of the chart to count how many students have collections of each item. (Students can be counted for more than one collection.) Then use the information to graph student hobbies.

Anna's Table by Eve Bunting. Northword Press, 2002. (K–2) Anna's Aunt Em gave her a table for her bedroom on which to put all the things from nature that she collects.

Collecting by Bonnie Dobkin. Scholastic Library Publishing, 1993. (K–1) It's so much fun to collect things that the boy wonders if he should quit. "Of course not, I told you—collecting is fun!" This Rookie Reader® includes a word list.

Hannah's Collections by Marthe Jocelyn. Dutton, 2000. (K–2) Hannah's collections are illustrated with mixed-media collage using the real items she collects and makes into a collage sculpture.

Josephina, the Great Collector by Diana Engel. William Morrow & Co., 1988. (K–2) Josephina's side of the bedroom becomes so overrun with her collection of random things that her sister is forced to sleep downstairs. In the end, Josephina uses her "junk" to make a very artistic tree house to share with her sister.

 # Collections

Duplicate a class set of the logic puzzle from page 37. Using the clues, have students place an "X" in the box when they determine that a person would not have that collection. Place a star in the box for the correct collection. Once a star is determined, remember to "X" all other boxes in the star's row and column.

For a more kinesthetic experience that saves paper and toner, mount a class set of logic puzzles on construction paper and laminate. Give each student a sandwich bag with black and white beans. Have them use the black beans as the "yes" markers and the white as "no" markers. After you share the answers, students return the beans to their bag and the set is ready for the next class.

Answers:

Lisa	buttons
Rupert	trading cards
Sylvester	rocks
Diana	bottle caps
Sasha	coins

 **Resources**

Books:

Anna's Table by Eve Bunting. Northword Press, 2002. (K–2) Anna's Aunt Em gave her a table for her bedroom on which to put all the things from nature that she collects.

Bunnies and Their Hobbies by Nancy Carlson. Lerner Publishing, 1984. (K–2) After work, bunnies do their chores and then enjoy their many hobbies.

Click! A Book About Cameras and Taking Pictures by Gail Gibbons. Little, Brown and Company, 1997. (K–3)

Coins **(Cool Collectibles)** by Jennifer Abeyta. Scholastic Library Publishing, 2000. (3–5) This series has 48 pages of high interest, easier reading information. Chapters explain what makes coins collectible, the history of U.S. coins, the value of coins and starting your own collection. Includes a glossary, index and bibliography.

Collecting by Bonnie Dobkin. Scholastic Library Publishing, 1993. (K–1) It's so much fun to collect things that the boy wonders if he should quit. "Of course not, I told you—collecting is fun!" This Rookie Reader® includes a word list.

Collecting Baseball Cards by Thomas S. Owens. Millbrook Press, 2000. (3–5) Students can learn how to start and enjoy the hobby, including how to survive a trade show, collect cards by mail, get autographs and spot counterfeits.

Collecting Basketball Cards by Thomas S. Owens. Millbrook Press, 1998. (3–5) Did you know that the first basketball cards, which came out in 1910, were printed on felt squares? Do you know the difference between a semi-star and a rookie player? Find out all about this combination of sport and hobby, including how and what to collect, how to tell the bonus from the bogus and how to get autographs and bargain cards. Includes an extensive glossary and index.

Dolls **(Cool Collectibles)** by Kristine Hooks. Scholastic Library Publishing, 2000. (3–5) The book begins with a history of dolls and includes which dolls are considered collectible. Throughout the book, there are interesting facts like, "The most valuable Barbie doll is a 1959 model, which is valued at more than $5,000." It includes a two-page glossary and index.

Hannah's Collections by Marthe Jocelyn. Dutton, 2000. (K–2) Hannah's collections are illustrated with mixed-media collage using the real items she collects and makes into a collage sculpture.

Josephina, the Great Collector by Diana Engel. William Morrow & Co., 1988. (K–2) Josephina's side of the bedroom becomes so overrun with her collection of random things that her sister is forced to sleep downstairs. In the end, Josephina uses her "junk" to make a very artistic tree house to share with her sister.

Military Collectibles **(Cool Collectibles)** by Patrick Newell. Scholastic Library Publishing, 2000. (3–5) This book begins with the story of a boy who collected over 100 unit patches during World War II. It goes on to explain what's collectible, such as medals, uniforms, insignia and badges and weapons. The last chapter tells where these items can be found and is followed by a timeline of wars involving the United States. Glossary, index and bibliography are included.

Miniature Cars **(Cool Collectibles)** by Julie Beyer. Scholastic Library Publishing, 2000. (3–5)

Picture This: Fun Photography and Crafts by Debra Friedman. Kids Can Press, 2003. (3–5)

Prudy's Problem and How She Solved It by Carey Armstrong-Ellis. Harry N. Abrams, 2002. (K–2) "All her friends had collections. And so did Prudy—but Prudy collected everything." After her room explodes from overcrowding, Prudy gets help to construct The Prudy Museum of Indescribable Wonderment.

Stamp Collecting by Neill Granger. Millbrook Press, 1994. (3–5) *Stamps* **(Cool Collectibles)** by Jennifer Abeyta. Scholastic Library Publishing, 2000. (3–5) Both titles give students information on the reasons and pleasures of the hobby along with an introduction that includes some of the history of stamp collecting. The Granger book is much more extensive and of more use to the interested collector.

Sylvester and the Magic Pebble by William Steig. Simon & Schuster, 1988. (K–3)

Trading Cards **(Cool Collectibles)** by Rob Kirkpatrick. Scholastic Library Publishing, 2000. (3–5) This is a brief overview of the hobby, with enough information to whet a child's interest and lead him or her to begin the hobby and select lengthier books for more information.

Web sites:

BabyAnt.com
www.babyant.com/bt037114.html
Order your plush 6" Sylvester by Crocodile Creek at this online baby super store. The cost is $9.50 plus shipping. It is also available at some independent bookstores.

Barbie® Collecting Start Page
www.collectdolls.about.com/library/blmenu2.htm?PM=ss16_collectdolls#Gen
Includes everything you'd want to know about America's Queen of the fashion dolls, and connects to all kinds of doll sites, including paper dolls, doll houses, doll making, restoration and how to identify and value your doll collection.

CoinMasters.org
www.coinmasters.org
Major links include Cybrary, Auction, Shows and Links, which include sites of dealers and hobbyists as well as useful information sites.

Junior Philatelists of America
www.jpastamps.org
Site includes everything to interest and help the young stamp collector.

Charting Collections

	Keychains	Shells	Sticker Books	Bells	Marbles	Cars	Pennies	Posters	Models	Stuffed Animals	Bugs/Bones	Baseball Cards	Comics	Sticks/Clothespins	Ribbons	Feathers	Buttons	Dolls	Barrettes	Stamps	Keys	Rocks
Boys in *Collecting*																						
Josephina																						
Hannah																						
Anna																						
Class Collections																						

Answer Key

	Keychains	Shells	Sticker Books	Bells	Marbles	Cars	Pennies	Posters	Models	Stuffed Animals	Bugs/Bones	Baseball Cards	Comics	Sticks/Clothespins	Ribbons	Feathers	Buttons	Dolls	Barrettes	Stamps	Keys	Rocks
Boys in *Collecting*	X	X	X	X	X	X	X	X	X	X	X	X	X									
Josephina		X												X	X	X	X					
Hannah		X								X	X			X		X	X	X	X	X		
Anna		X									X					X						X
Class Collections																						

Collections Logic Puzzle

Can you match each child to his or her collection? Place an "X" in the box when you determine that a person does not collect that item. Place a star in the box for the correct item. Once a star is determined, remember to "X" all of the boxes in the star's row and column.

	Coins	Trading Cards	Buttons	Rocks	Bottle Caps
Lisa					
Rupert					
Sylvester					
Diana					
Sasha					

Clues

1. Lisa's collection comes in handy when she sews.

2. Diana likes her collection because it helps recycle what might be discarded.

3. Sylvester collects the same thing as the book character with his name.

4. Sasha is afraid he will spend his collection by accident.

Teddy Bear Day

Teddy bears are wonderful reminders for us to have soft edges, be full of love and trust and always ready for a hug.

–Author unknown

Making a Teddy Bear

MAIN ACTIVITY

Grades: K–2 (Grades 3–5 can use the game activity to learn the history of the teddy bear and facts about some famous bears.)

Purposes:

- To sequence steps in making a teddy bear.

- To learn the origin and history of teddy bears.

- To celebrate National Teddy Bear Day (November 14).

Format: Nonfiction Read Aloud, Individual Sequencing Activity

Materials:

- variety of stuffed bears

- *How Teddy Bears Are Made: A Visit to the Vermont Teddy Bear Factory* by Ann Morris (Scholastic, 1994)

- class set of sequence card envelopes from page 46

Prepare in Advance: Reproduce the sequence cards for each student. Make a transparency of page 46. Cut apart the copies and put them into an envelope for each set. Locate bears. Bring in a variety of sizes, colors and types of stuffed bears.

Activity Directions:

1. Show your bears and encourage discussion. Ask students if they know how the bears were made. Using a chalk or white board, list the steps as students name them for you.

2. Read aloud *How Teddy Bears Are Made: A Visit to the Vermont Teddy Bear Factory,* a true book that shows how bears are made at the Vermont Teddy Bear Factory.

3. After the reading, revisit the list generated by students, adding or eliminating steps.

4. Give each child an envelope of pictures and ask them to put the pictures in sequence.

5. Display the transparency and have the students check their work. Then ask them to scramble the pictures before putting them back into the envelopes.

Shower Curtain Jeopardy Board

Materials:

- 1 opaque solid-color shower curtain liner

- 1 roll of heavy-duty clear tape, wide

- 1 roll of narrow clear Scotch tape

- 30 sheet protectors, heavy duty

- 30 sheets of card stock, 6 sheets of 5 colors

- 1 pair of small, sharp scissors

- computer and printer or a black marker

Directions:

1. Lay out the curtain liner on a large flat surface. I use my dining room table.

2. Cut five of the page protectors in half. Keep the bottom halves.

3. For the other 25, cut a "V" or a "U" in the front edge of the top to make the removal of inserted cards easier. The cut should extend from side to side and be no deeper than ⅓ of the page protector.

4. Along the far left edge of the curtain, begin at the bottom and lay five page protectors in a column, spaced an inch apart and 1½" from the outside edge. At the top of the column place the half pocket. When the pockets appear evenly spaced, hold them in place with a small piece of Scotch tape on each side so they won't slide.

5. Leave an inch between the first column and the next. Repeat step 3, making sure the pockets appear even both vertically and horizontally.

6. When the first two columns are tacked down and even, run a strip of the wide tape from the top to the bottom of the first column on both sides.

7. Repeat steps 3–5 as you lay down each column until all five columns are adhered lengthwise.

8. Next, run rows of tape from side to side, beginning with the tops of the half pockets.

9. When all of the rows have been adhered, use scissors to cut the tape at the top edges of the pockets so the game cards will slide in and out easily.

10. Use a marker or computer/printer to make the card stock into game cards. Each color should have the prices written on the front and the back. The front of the cards should say $10, $20, $30, $40 and $50. The backs should say $100, $200, $300, $400, $500.

11. Print column topics on card stock, using a half sheet of card stock. Slide them into the top row.

12. The answers can be printed on white paper that will be hidden under the amount cards and revealed when they are pulled from the pocket in response to a contestant.

 ## "Teddy Bears' Picnic"

"The Teddy Bears' Picnic" is a fun song to sing. HarperCollins has published a version that includes illustrations by Bruce Whatley and a cassette of the song arranged and performed by Jerry Garcia and David Grisman. As a prize for a bear contest we had, the winners (K–2) had lunch provided in the library. They were invited to bring a teddy with them, and we shared this book and song before we ate.

Act out some of these traditional bear chants and songs.

"Fuzzy Wuzzy"

Fuzzy Wuzzy was a bear.
Fuzzy Wuzzy had no hair.
If Fuzzy Wuzzy had no hair,
Then Fuzzy Wuzzy wasn't fuzzy,
Was he?

"The Bear Went Over the Mountain" Song
(Sung to the tune: "For He's a Jolly Good Fellow")

The bear went over the mountain,
The bear went over the mountain,
The bear went over the mountain,
To see what he could see.

To see what he could see,
To see what he could see.
The bear went over the mountain,
To see what he could see.

The other side of the mountain,
The other side of the mountain,
The other side of the mountain,
Was all that he could see.

Was all that he could see,
Was all that he could see.
The other side of the mountain,
Was all that he could see!

"Teddy Bear, Teddy Bear"

Teddy bear, teddy bear, turn around.
Teddy bear, teddy bear, touch the ground.
Teddy bear, teddy bear, show your shoe.
Teddy bear, teddy bear, that will do!
Teddy bear, teddy bear, go upstairs.
Teddy bear, teddy bear, say your prayers.
Teddy bear, teddy bear, turn out the light.
Teddy bear, teddy bear, say goodnight!

 # We're Going on a Bear Hunt

Read Michael Rosen and Helen Oxenbury's version (Simon & Schuster, 1989) of this traditional story. Help children enact the bear hunt either during or after the reading. Use the following gestures as you read:

For the refrain:

We're going on a bear hunt. *(Hand above eyes as if searching.)*
We're going to catch a big one. *(Arms spread to show size of bear.)*
What a beautiful day. *(Palms up.)*
We're not scared! *(Cross arms and shake head with a fierce look.)*

For the lines, use these gestures:

Oh no! *(Slap head gently.)*
We can't go under it, *(Hands dive under.)*
Can't go over it, *(Hands dive up.)*
We'll have to go around it. *(Spread arms as if to encircle something.)*

Act out the other adventures as well, when they go through the grass, river, mud, forest and even a snowstorm until they reach the cave. After discovering the bear, reverse all of the actions in fast motion until everyone is safe under the covers in bed.

 # Bear Jeopardy

Make the game per the instructions for the Shower Curtain Jeopardy Board on page 39. Or make an overhead transparency of page 49. As a team selects their category and amount, unmask one of the questions on pages 47–48. Be sure children see the answers rather than just hear you read them, so they can make smart guesses.

Answer Key

Most answers can be found in *Famous Bears and Friends: One Hundred Years of Stories, Poems, Songs, and Heroics* by Janet Coleman (Dutton, 2002).

American Bears

The teddy bear is named for / *b. President Theodore Roosevelt*

The American teddy bear was invented in 1902 in / *c. Brooklyn, New York*

The idea for the stuffed toy bear was inspired by / *d. a hunting incident*

The makers of the first American teddy bears were / *d. owners of a candy store*

The first toy bears in America were made by a company called / *a. Ideal*

German Bears

The stuffed teddy bear was invented / *a. 100 years ago*

Toy bears were invented in 1903 in Germany by / *a. the nephew of a crippled toy maker*

German bears were made by a company called / *d. Steiff Toy Company*

The Germans called their stuffed bears / *c. Bear dolls*

German bears were different from teddy bears because / *c. their arms and legs could move*

Winnie the Pooh

Winnie the Pooh was written by / *d. A. A. Milne*

Winnie the Pooh stories began as / *b. bedtime stories*

The owner of Winnie the Pooh, in the book and real life, is / *d. Christopher Robin (Milne)*

Winnie the Pooh got his name from / *a. an army mascot and a swan*

Winnie's friends were Christopher's other toys. Which is not one of them? / *c. Rabbit (a Disney addition)*

Famous Bears

Paddington Bear was originally / *a. a gift to the author's wife*

Which of the following is not true? / *d. some type of teddy bear is found in every room of the White House*

The toy store bear that lost his overalls button is / *c. Corduroy*

The Berenstain Bears are written by Jan and Stan Berenstain. They are / *b. husband and wife*

A famous bear song begins, "If you go down in the woods today, you're sure of a big surprise." What are the bears doing in the woods that is surprising? / *c. having a picnic*

Bear Facts

Which is the largest member of the bear family? / *b. polar bear*

What color is a polar bear's skin? / *c. black*

Which of the following is not eaten by bears? / *c. garbage*

Which bear does not hibernate? / *d. polar bear*

Which of the following is not true? / *c. bears have three cubs in the spring (usually only 1 or 2)*

Name the Bear Character

Use book jackets, calendar pages or book character dolls to feature a variety of book bears. Give students an entry form that contains a number and blank for each bear. Supply a list of answers, with one more bear name than in the display. Students who get 80% of the names correct are entered in a drawing for bear bookmarks, books or a stuffed bear.

 **Resources**

Books:

Bears: Paws, Claws, and Jaws by Adele D. Richardson and Lola M. Schaefer. Capstone Press, 2001. (1–3) The left side of the book contains full-page color spreads of the eight kinds of bears. The facing pages have large print sentences. Fun facts are contained in boxes, and each page has a word that is defined at the bottom, like habitat and warm-blooded. A simple glossary, index and suggestions for additional reading and Internet sites are appended.

The Boy Who Thought He Was a Teddy Bear: A Fairy Tale by Jeanne Willis. Peachtree Publishers, 2002. (K–2) Edward, a little boy, lives in the woods with the Three Teddy Bears, walking, talking and moving just like a bear. But even though he loves acting like a teddy bear, he sometimes wonders what it would be like to be a little boy.

Famous Bears and Friends: One Hundred Years of Stories, Poems, Songs, and Heroics written and collected by Janet Wyman Coleman. Dutton, 2002. (2–5). Beginning with the story of Teddy Roosevelt and the Michtoms, Ms. Coleman gives us the history behind the book story of Winnie the Pooh (including photos of A. A. Milne's son, Christopher Robin, with the teddy bear model), Paddington Bear and Corduroy. Here you'll find the words and music to "The Teddy Bears' Picnic." Readers will discover that teddy bears were retrieved from the *Titanic,* have made 400 jumps with the Royal Military Academy's Parachuting Club and been to space on the space shuttle *Discovery.* There is even a Japanese robot bear named Kuma who can wiggle, sing, talk (in Japanese) and smile.

Goldilocks and the Three Bears retold by Jan Brett. Putnam, 1987. (K–3) Richly illustrated, this traditional version is adapted from The Green Fairy Book and brings the bears warmly to life and emphasizes their family love.

How Teddy Bears Are Made: A Visit to the Vermont Teddy Bear Factory by Ann Morris. Scholastic, 1994. (K–3) Clear color photos show a variety of workers who design, cut, sew, stuff, dress, box and take orders. Looking at the photos of the factory and the workers is like taking a field trip and the text is easily understood.

The Hutchinson Treasury of Teddy Bear Tales. Hutchinson, 1997. (1–3) This collection contains 12 beloved teddy stories, including "Little Bear Lost" (Jane Hissey), "Ruby" (Maggie Glen) and "Teddybears on Stage" (Susana Gretz). Many of the others are favorites in England, and will be new to American readers. Original illustrations are included.

Jesse Bear, What Will You Wear? by Nancy White Carlstrom. Simon & Schuster, 1996. (K–2) Follow Jesse Bear though his day with verse and Bruce Degen's humorous illustrations. As he leaves the house, Jesse is wearing his shirt, and "I'll wear my pants, My pants that dance, My pants that dance in the morning." There are several more books about Jesse Bear.

Know-It-Alls: Bears! by Christopher Nicholas. Learning Horizons, Inc., 2000. (K–2) Crammed with facts about the eight kinds of bears, though there are no more than four sentences on a page. Fact boxes, large colorful format and questions as section headings ("What do bears eat?) make this of great interest to budding naturalists.

The Legend of the Teddy Bear by Frank Murphy. Sleeping Bear Press, 2000. (K–5) Author's note includes facts about Roosevelt, but none about the Michtoms. In this version, they decide to make bears so children could hug them while sleeping. This and *A Teddy Bear for President Roosevelt* include the incident where they send a bear to the president with a request to use his name. Both include a fictional letter that is similar in spirit.

My Friend Bear by Jez Alborough. Candlewick Press, 1998. (K–2) Eddie and Bear cling to their teddy bears when they are frightened at the sight of one another. This gets them giggling, and they, and their teddies become fast friends.

The Teddy Bear Encyclopedia by Pauline Cockrill. DK Publishing, 2001. (3–5) This 240-page book is lavishly illustrated with color photographs, and covers the history of teddy bears from the Steiff and Michtom (Ideal Toy Company) bears to today's mass-market collectibles. Arranged as a catalog with four bears to a page, children can see the variety of bodies, faces and materials used to make these beloved bears. It ends with chapters on arctophily (collecting bears) and the care and repair of bears.

A Teddy Bear for President Roosevelt by Connie and Peter Roop. Scholastic, 2002. (K–3) An easy chapter book that explains the Michtom's need to make a bear like they knew from Russia in order to prove they are proud Americans and to help pay the rent on their candy store. They receive a letter from President Roosevelt giving them permission to use his name, but it is a fictional letter. Compare with *The Legend of the Teddy Bear.* Includes an author's note with the facts.

The Teddy Bears' Picnic performed by Jerry Garcia and David Grisman. HarperCollins, 1999. (K–2) David Whatley's large double-spread illustrations are perfect for the younger crowd. Phrases of the song are illustrated on each page ("You better go in disguise" is illustrated with bears wearing pig noses).

Teddy Bear Tears by Jim Aylesworth. Simon & Schuster, 1997. (K–2) A small boy comforts his four teddy bears, Willie Bear, Fuzzy, Ringo and Little Sam, who each have fears in the night. As he does so, the boy makes the night worry-free for himself as well. The colored pencil illustrations are warm and cuddly.

We're Going on a Bear Hunt by Michael Rosen; illustrated by Helen Oxenbury. Simon & Schuster, 1989. (K–2)

Web sites:

The Bear Den—Species by Species
www.bearden.org/species.html
Click on any of the eight species to read its description, range, habitat, diet, social organization and reproduction. Also indicated are the bear's conservation status and threats to its survival.

The Story of the Teddy Bear

www.theodoreroosevelt.org/kidscorner/tr_teddy.htm

Learn the brief facts of the creation of Teddy's bear and see the political cartoon that began the teddy's life.

Teddy Bear Story—100 Years of the Teddy Bear

www.liverpoolmuseum.org.uk/teddies

Click on a selection of interesting topics including Bears in Books, Bear Beginnings and Showbiz Bears.

Making a Teddy Bear

A bear designer draws a pattern.

The pattern is made into a large metal die like a cookie cutter.

A big machine stamps out the parts of the bear.

Ears, arms and legs are sewn by hand on a sewing machine.

Stuffing is blown into the bear's head, arms and legs.

The body stuffing is put in by hand.

The back of the bear is sewn closed.

The bear's fur is brushed.

The bear is dressed.

The bear tag is attached.

The bear is carefully packed and mailed.

The bear is bought and taken home!

THIS TEDDY BEAR WAS MADE WITH ♥

Bear Jeopardy

Bears

The teddy bear is named for

a. Amanda Teddy

b. President Theodore Roosevelt

c. Teddy Smith

d. Thomas "Teddy" Bayer

The American teddy bear was invented in 1902 in

a. Austin, Texas

b. San Francisco, California

c. Brooklyn, New York

d. Washington, D.C.

The idea for the stuffed toy bear was inspired by

a. a sick child in a hospital

b. a new bear cub at the St. Louis zoo

c. a contest for a new toy

d. a hunting incident

The makers of the first American teddy bears were

a. makers of wooden trains

b. pet store owners

c. friends of orphaned wildlife

d. owners of a candy store

The first toy bears in America were made by a company called

a. Ideal

b. Mattel

c. Hasbro

d. Parker Brothers

German Bears

The stuffed teddy bear was invented

a. 100 years ago

b. 200 years ago

c. 500 years ago

d. 1,000 years ago

Toy bears were invented in 1903 in Germany by

a. the nephew of a crippled toy maker

b. the mother of a dog lover

c. a keeper at the Stuttgart zoo

d. a high school girl for a sewing class

German bears were made by a company called

a. Berlin Child Crafts

b. Kinder Bears

c. Tannenbaum Toys

d. Steiff Toy Company

The Germans called their stuffed bears

a. Rudolph bears

b. Kinder bears

c. Bear dolls

d. Beirniken

German bears were different from teddy bears because

a. they had cloth skin instead of fur

b. they had cloth eyes instead of button eyes

c. their arms and legs could move

d. they had necks and tails

Winnie the Pooh

Winnie the Pooh was written by

a. Stan Berenstain

b. J. J. Alborough

c. Jan Brett

d. A. A. Milne

Winnie the Pooh stories began as

a. campfire stories

b. bedtime stories

c. TV cartoons

d. songs for babies

The owner of Winnie the Pooh, in the book and real life, is
a. Sally Ann
b. Martin Luther
c. John Henry
d. Christopher Robin

Winnie the Pooh got his name from
a. an army mascot and a swan
b. a famous actress and a dog
c. the British prime minister and a child's game
d. a popular French cartoon character

Winnie's friends were Christopher's other toys. Which is not one of them?
a. Tigger
b. Kanga
c. Rabbit
d. Eeyore

Famous Bears

Paddington Bear was originally
a. a gift to the author's wife
b. made by the author's daughter
c. a dream that came to the author while camping
d. written for grown-ups

Which of the following is not true?
a. a teddy bear was found in the pocket of a dead *Titanic* crew member
b. a British military parachuting group jumps with a teddy bear
c. a bear was on board the space shuttle *Discovery*
d. some type of teddy bear is found in every room of the White House

The toy store bear that lost his overalls button is
a. Paddington Bear
b. Winnie the Pooh
c. Corduroy
d. My Friend Bear

The Berenstain Bears are written by Jan and Stan Berenstain. They are
a. brother and sister
b. husband and wife
c. mother and son
d. cousins

A famous bear song begins, "If you go down in the woods today, you're sure of a big surprise." What are the bears doing in the woods that is surprising?
a. having a pool party
b. practicing ballet
c. having a picnic
d. learning to ride horses

Bear Facts

Which is the largest member of the bear family?
a. grizzly bear
b. polar bear
c. Asian sun bear
d. black bear

What color is a polar bear's skin?
a. white
b. pink
c. black
d. brown

Which of the following is not eaten by bears?
a. meat
b. fruit
c. garbage
d. insects

Which bear does not hibernate?
a. black bear
b. grizzly bear
c. spectacled bear
d. polar bear

Which of the following is not true?
a. Bears can run fast.
b. Bears can climb trees.
c. Bears have three cubs in the spring.
d. Bears have an excellent sense of smell.

Bear Jeopardy

American Bears	German Bears	Famous Bears	Winnie the Pooh	Bear Facts
10	10	10	10	10
20	20	20	20	20
30	30	30	30	30
40	40	40	40	40
50	50	50	50	50

Winter

If we had no winter, the spring would not be as pleasant
–Anne Bradstreet

Persephone and Demeter

Grades: 3–5

Purpose:

- To learn about the Greek mythical explanation for winter and the change of seasons.

Format: Share a Greek Myth through Hearing and Drawing

Materials:

- globe or world map

- flashlight

- selection of Greek and Roman myth books

- one of the titles listed with the activity directions

- crayons, pencils and drawing paper for students

- Web site listed in activity directions available on student computers or projected for class use *(optional)*

Prepare in Advance: Display the books. Hang a map or display globe. Bookmark the myth of Persephone in selected books. Set up a computer projector if using the Web site. Gather drawing materials.

Activity Directions:

1. Explain the scientific reason for the season, using one of the winter books in your collection if desired or *The Nature and Science of Winter* by Jane Burton and Kim Taylor (Gareth Stevens, 1999). Use the globe and a flashlight to illustrate if desired. The winter solstice, or first day of winter, is the day the earth is leaning farthest away from the sun and when the daylight is the shortest.

2. The ancient Greeks and Romans had no way to scientifically discover the earth's tilt, so they created a myth to explain the changing of seasons. Share with students a version of the myth of Demeter and Persephone. Use a book from your collection, or one of the titles or the Web site listed below.

   Gods and Goddesses from Greek Myths by Pat Posner. McGraw-Hill Children's Publishing, 2003. (3–5)

   Greek Gods and Heroes by Robert Graves. Bantam Doubleday Dell, 1973. (5)

   The New York Public Library Amazing Mythology: A Book of Answers for Kids by the New York Public Library and Brendan January. John Wiley and Sons, 2000. (5)

   Persephone and the Pomegranate: A Myth from Greece by Kris Waldherr. Penguin Putnam, 1993. (3–5)

   Story of Persephone
   www.windows.ucar.edu/tour/link=/mythology/persephone_seasons.html&edu=high

3. If time allows, have students illustrate either the scientific explanation for winter or the mythological version. Display illustrations on a bulletin board that says "Winter Arrives." Beneath it, display your myth books, as well as fiction and nonfiction books about winter.

 # Snowballs and *Tacky the Penguin*

Sharing Reader's Theater can enliven winter days. Try one of the scripts below. Read them with younger classes, or have older students read them to younger students.

Snowballs *Reader's Theater Script*
www.readinglady.com/Readers_Theater/Scripts/Snowballs.doc
Snowballs (by Lois Ehlert with a script by Sandy Tuttle) is for nine readers in first or second grade.

Tacky the Penguin *Reader's Theater Script*
www.readinglady.com/Readers_Theater/Scripts/Tacky_the_Penguin.doc
Tacky thrives in the cold of the winter, but has trouble conforming to his penguin friends. *Tacky the Penguin* by Helen Lester (Houghton Mifflin, 1988) is for 15 readers.

 # Seasonal Tic-Tac-Toe

See page 23.

 # Winter Breaks

The Mystery Master Logic Puzzle

www.mysterymaster.com/puzzles/WinterBreaks.html

Five men from different parts of the country each chose to go on a winter-sports holiday in a different area. While skiing, each had an accident in which he suffered a fracture of a different part of his anatomy. From the clues given at this site, can you work out who lives in which town, where he went for his holiday and what he broke?

 # Identify Animal Tracks and Cultural Celebrations

Animal Tracks

www.leslietryon.com/animals1101/animalfootprints.html

Use the tracks at this site to identify animals that hunt for food in the winter. Use with *In the Snow: Who's Been Here?* by Lindsay George (Greenwillow Books, 1995).

Winter Celebrations: WebQuest for Second Grade

jets.utep.edu/helen_ball/awauson/winter/adriawauson/index.htm

Learn about various cultures and how they celebrate their winter holidays.

 # Resources

Books:

Bear Snores On by Karma Wilson. Simon & Schuster, 2001. (K–2) The animals take refuge in bear's cave, but he is none too happy to be awakened by their antics.

A Cold Day by Lola M. Schaefer. Capstone Press, 1999. (K–1)

Cold Days by Jennifer Burke. Scholastic Library Publishing, 2000. (2–4)

First Snow by Helen Coutant. Knopf, 1974. (K–2) The metaphor of winter following the growing seasons helps Lien to understand her grandmother's death.

Gods and Goddesses from Greek Myths by Pat Posner. McGraw-Hill Children's Publishing, 2003. (3–5)

Greek Gods and Heroes by Robert Graves. Bantam Doubleday Dell, 1973. (5)

In the Snow: Who's Been Here? by Lindsay George. Greenwillow Books, 1995. (2–5)

Muwin and the Magic Hare by Susan Hand Shetterly. Simon & Schuster, 1993. (3–5) This Native American folktale tells of Muwin the bear and the stories he hears from his friend just before he takes his winter nap.

The Nature and Science of Winter by Jane Burton and Kim Taylor. Gareth Stevens, 1999. (3–5)

The New York Public Library Amazing Mythology: A Book of Answers for Kids by the New York Public Library and Brendan January. John Wiley and Sons, 2000. (5)

Persephone and the Pomegranate: A Myth from Greece by Kris Waldherr. Penguin Putnam, 1993. (3–5)

Poppleton in Winter by Cynthia Rylant. Blue Sky Press, 2001. (1–3)

Snowballs by Lois Ehlert. Harcourt, 1995. (K–2)

A Snowy Day by Lola M. Schaefer. Capstone Press, 1999. (K–1)

The Snowy Day by Ezra Jack Keats. Viking, 1998. (K–2) Peter enjoys playing in the snow in this Caldecott winner.

Snow is Falling by Franklyn Branley. HarperCollins, 2000. (2–4)

Tacky the Penguin by Helen Lester. Houghton Mifflin, 1988. (K–3)

Warm Clothes by Gail Saunders-Smith. Capstone Press, 1997. (K–1)

Winter by Terri DeGezelle. Capstone Press, 2002. (K–2)

Winter by Gail Saunders-Smith. Capstone Press, 1998. (K–1)

Winter by Darlene Stille. Compass Point Books, 2001. (1–3)

Winter: An Alphabet Acrostic by Steven Schnur. Clarion Books, 2002. (2–5) Acrostic poetry that captures the sights, sounds and smells of winter.

Winter: Signs of the Season Around North America by Mary Pat Finnegan. Picture Window Books, 2002. (1–3)

Winter Wood by David Spohn. HarperCollins, 1991. (2–3) Matt and his dad chop wood, chat and observe the birds and changes of winter.

Web sites:

Animal Tracks
www.leslietryon.com/animals1101/animalfootprints.html

The Mystery Master Logic Puzzle
www.mysterymaster.com/puzzles/WinterBreaks.html

Snowballs ***Reader's Theater Script***
www.readinglady.com/Readers_Theater/Scripts/Snowballs.doc

Story of Persephone
www.windows.ucar.edu/tour/link=/mythology/persephone_seasons.html&edu=high

Tacky the Penguin ***Reader's Theater Script***
www.readinglady.com/Readers_Theater/Scripts/Tacky_the_Penguin.doc

Winter Celebrations: WebQuest for Second Grade
jets.utep.edu/helen_ball/awauson/winter/adriawauson/index.htm

Winter Crafts
www.enchantedlearning.com/crafts/winter/
Includes simple crafts, cards, shape books, winter stories and much more.

Winter Fun Links to Learning
www.mikids.com/winterfun.html
Activities include Bounce the Penguin, Snowball Skiball, Find the Icy Match, Snowboard Mount Fiji, Polar Pairs, Real Snowflakes and more.

Winter Online Games
www.kidsdomain.com/games/winter.html
Thirty-seven games include Building Snowmen, X-Treme Snowboarding and Ice Bowling.

The Winter Solstice
www.mikids.com/december.html
Test Your Knowledge: Winter Solstice Traditions Quiz, Winter Solstice Quiz, Myths About Ancient Sun Gods, Holiday Activities and Top Ten Cures for Cabin Fever.

Celebrating Firsts

Life begins as a quest of the child for the man and ends as a journey by the man to rediscover the child.
–Laurens Van der Post

Remembering the Firsts

Grades: K–5

Purposes:

- To note progress by remembering the firsts of our lives.

- To share emotions with others as we talk about the courage, fear and curiosity that often marks our first experiences.

Format: Group Discussion, Book Sharing

Materials:

- blackboard, chart tablet or other writing surface with which to share children's responses

- variety of books about "firsts" (see pages 58–59)

- bookmark for each child

Prepare in Advance: Set up writing materials. Pull and display books. Duplicate a bookmark for each child.

Activity Directions:

1. Ask students if they think they have pretty good memories. Tell them that we will be talking about the first time they did something they may be good at now, or something they may take for granted. Ask them to think about such an experience, whether it happened in their early years or just last week. Some of the experiences might have been scary, some might have satisfied their curiosity and some might have made them feel successful and happy.

2. Head several columns with these emotions: fearful, brave, curious, silly and determined. Then have students briefly suggest an activity that made them feel that way the first time they did it.

3. After students have listed and discussed their first-time memories, tell them they deserve recognition for taking so many risks. Give each a bookmark to complete about firsts they are proud of.

4. Share one of the resource books with students. It can be a springboard for students to relive their own experiences. Writing about them is a good follow-up activity in the classroom.

 Me First

Me First *Reader's Theater Script*
www.readinglady.com/Readers_Theater/Scripts/mefirst.doc
Firsts can be exciting and admirable when they involve curiosity or courage. However, when selfishness is involved, as it is with Pinkerton the Pig who always has to be first, there's another lesson to be learned. The script for *Me First* by Helen Lester (Houghton Mifflin, 1992) is adapted by Laura Kump and has eight readers.

Game Day

Rather than making New Year's Resolutions, celebrate all the firsts that students have accomplished by having a Game Day. Select educational games you have for students to play in small groups. Or bring games from home, solicit games from students or play several class games. Students will take turns being "first," and it may be the first time they have played this particular game, or played a game with this group of students.

See the Computer Activity on page 57 for online games that students can play as partners. You can order educational games such as *Library Trivia Quest* and *Dewey®Match?* from Highsmith.

Beginners

Duplicate a class set of the logic puzzle on page 60. Using the clues, have students place an "X" in the box when they determine that a person would not be likely to undertake that activity. Place a star if that is the correct activity. Once a star is determined, remember to "X" all other boxes in the star's row and column.

For a more kinesthetic experience that saves paper and toner, mount a class set of logic puzzles on construction paper and laminate. Give each student a sandwich bag with black and white beans. Have them use the black beans as the "yes" markers and the white as "no" markers. After you share the answers, students return the beans to their bag and the set is ready for the next class.

Solution: Joey kicked a soccer goal; Lane got a tetanus shot; Pat flew a model plane; Kelly tried Rollerblades; and Jack typed an e-mail.

First Lines

"There is no lake at Camp Green Lake."* Do you recognize which book begins with this intriguing line? A story or book's first line is crucial. Many readers will discard a book after reading only the first line. But if an author can hook a young reader with the first sentence, he or she may be able to reel the reader in to the very end.

Have a contest in which you provide students with a list of first lines and the books from which they came. Their task is to match the line with the book title. Set a deadline for entries to be turned into the library. After the deadline, check the papers. All who get 80% or more correct (or whatever percentage you decide) will be entered in a grade level drawing. Award prizes to at least one winner from each grade.

For ten groups of first lines, five primary sets and five intermediate sets, go to Kathy Vandergrift's Web site, First Lines, at **scils.rutgers.edu/%7Ekvander/firstlinesindex.html.**

Use the lists as they are and have teams take turns choosing a first line, guessing the book and earning or losing points with each question. Or write the first lines and titles on a worksheet on which students can match the book with the quote. (*Holes* by Louis Sachar.)

Games Online

Hangman
superkids.com/aweb/tools/words/hangman
This variation of the popular word game can be played with topics like U.S. presidents, geography, famous cartoons and sports.

JigZone
www.jigzone.com
Click and drag the pieces to assemble the puzzle picture. Choose the number of pieces wanted in the puzzle, including 6, 22, 35, 48, 70, 100 or 240. Choose the shape of the pieces. Then select the picture to assemble. A timer lets you know how long it took to assemble, and a click will assemble the puzzle if one gets frustrated.

Kids' Place Games
eduplace.com/kids/games.html
These excellent games are fun and educational. Fake Out teaches new words, GeoNet develops geography skills and Wacky Web Tales encourages creative word choices similar to Mad Libs.

Mancala
imagiware.com/mancala
This is an easily learned strategy game that is addictive. It is based on a traditional African game. Students can play against one another or the computer.

Room 108 Games
www.scugog-net.com/room108/starflight/games1.html
Students can play 25 games, including electronic versions of Battleship, Dominoes, Rubik's Cube, Checkers, MasterMind, Connect 4 and Tetris.

 # Resources

Books:

As Big As You by Elaine Greenstein. Random House, 2002. (K–2) (First days of life.) Every other page is filled with similes comparing the baby to a variety of plants, fruits and vegetables ("your fingertips as sweet as raspberries"). Its actions are compared to baby animals.

Don't Go by Jane Breskin Zalben. Clarion Books, 2001. (K–1) (First day of preschool.) The story of an elephant child's anxiety at being separated from his mother is told with warm illustrations and followed by tips to parents about making that first day better for both. Daniel's Pumpkin Vanilla-Chip Cookies recipe ends the book.

First Friends by Lenore Blegvad. HarperCollins, 2000. (K) In a play-school situation, the reader meets a boy who has a block and a little girl who has a clock. Twelve children have 12 things. After the center illustration, which shows them in their playroom, the children interact. "I'll show you my block. Come and hear my clock!" and so make their first friends.

First Lessons in Ballet by Lise Friedman. Workman Publishing, 1999. (3–5) From warming up to stepping out, students can learn about the various positions and steps (photos include girls and boys) of beginning ballet. The French terms are explained along with their phonetic pronunciation.

First Riding Lessons by Sandy Ransford. Houghton Mifflin, 2002. (3–5) Even those without a horse will learn a great deal and can experience the lessons through the clear photographs and chapters called "Before you Start," "A Pony's Tack," "First Lessons," "In the Arena" and "Looking Forward" (safety, trail riding and competitive riding). Includes a glossary and index.

Going to the Dentist by Helen Frost. Capstone Press, 1999. (K–2) Though not one's favorite experience, the first time one goes to the dentist involves both courage and curiosity. The clear photos and simple language clarify what happens on such a trip.

Hatchet by Gary Paulsen. Atheneum, 1987. (3–5) Thirteen-year-old Brian survives one "first" after another, beginning with the death of his small plane pilot as they are in mid-flight to Alaska. Brian uses his wits and courage to deal with his fears and the variety of difficulties he faces.

Jingle Dancer by Cynthia Leitich Smith. William Morrow & Co., 2000. (3–5) (First traditional dance.) Jenna is a member of the Muscogee (Creek) Nation in Oklahoma and is old enough to join the women in dancing her first jingle dance. She borrows jingle cones from family and friends to sew on her dress so it can gain its voice. This contemporary story of a Native American demonstrates the support of family and community. An author's note and glossary are appended. Relevant information is provided at the author's Web site: **www.cyn thialeitichsmith.com.**

"Let's Get a Pup!" Said Kate by Bob Graham. Candlewick Press, 2001. (2–4) (First dog.)

Me First by Helen Lester. Houghton Mifflin, 1992. (K–2)

One, Two, Skip a Few! First Number Rhymes by Roberta Arenson. Barefoot Books, 1998. (K–2) Children will remember the excitement of learning to count. Relive that with these traditional counting and number rhymes that are cheerily illustrated.

Out and About at the Bakery by Jennifer A. Ericsson. Picture Window Books, 2002. (K–3) Part of the Field Trips series that also includes trips to the apple orchard, dairy farm, fire station, orchestra and zoo.

Potty Time by Guido Van Genechten. Simon & Schuster, 2001. (K) This book from Belgium has large humorous illustrations showing a variety of animals sitting on a potty. "'Here's a potty for my great big bottom,' said Nellie Elephant with a thump." Giraffe has a neat little bottom, pig a round pink bottom, etc., until Joe sits on it and it is perfect for his bottom.

Teammates by Peter Golenbock. Harcourt, 1990. (3–5) When teams were "whites only," it took tremendous courage to be both the first black player on the team and the first white player to be his friend and teammate.

Tiny Rabbit Goes to a Birthday Party by John Wallace. Holiday House, 2000. (K–2) What to wear? What gift to get? How to wrap it? What if I don't know anyone? Tiny Rabbit is a bit reluctant to join in at first, but then has so much fun that he can't wait to get home and plan his own birthday party.

Web sites:

First Lines
scils.rutgers.edu/%7Ekvander/firstlinesindex.html

Hangman
superkids.com/aweb/tools/words/hangman

JigZone
www.jigzone.com

Kids' Place Games
eduplace.com/kids/games.html

Mancala
imagiware.com/mancala

Me First ***Reader's Theater Script***
www.readinglady.com/Readers_Theater/Scripts/mefirst.doc

Room 108 Games
www.scugog-net.com/room108/starflight/games1.html

Beginners Logic Puzzle

Can you match each child to his or her "firsts"? Place an "X" in the box when you determine that a person would not have done the activity. Place a star in the box for the correct activity. Once a star is determined, remember to "X" all of the boxes in the star's row and column.

	Typed an e-mail.	Got a tetanus shot.	Tried Roller-blades.	Flew a model plane.	Kicked a soccer goal.
Joey					
Lane					
Pat					
Kelly					
Jack					

Clues

1. Joey was outside for his first try.

2. Pat has always loved flying and Kelly skated over to watch the plane race.

3. Lane's experience was painful.

Library Lovers Month

I love the place; the magnificent books; I require books as I require air.
–Sholem Asch, referring to the library

The Library Dragon Reader's Theater

 MAIN ACTIVITY

Grades: 2–5

Purpose:

- To use voice in retelling a story through reader's theater.

Format: Reader's Theater and/or Read Aloud

Materials:

- *The Library Dragon* by Carmen Agra Deedy (Peachtree Publishers, 1994)

- script from pages 67–70

- character signs from pages 71–72

Prepare in Advance: Make enough copies of the script for all of your readers, plus one for you and one for the teacher. On each copy, highlight the speaker's name and all of his or her lines. Make character signs for each student. Reproduce pages 71–72 on card stock, enlarging if desired. Color the illustrations. Cut the signs apart and mount them on tongue depressors.

Activity Directions:

1. Explain to students that in Reader's Theater, there are no costumes, props, scenery, makeup or special effects. Each actor has only his or her voice to show the character's personality. Discuss the ways one can use voice to show emotion and give examples.

2. Ask the teacher to appoint 15 readers, have the students volunteer for selected parts or distribute the scripts randomly.

3. Tell the students to read their highlighted parts silently, thinking how they will use their voice inflection and intonation to show emotion and humor. Help students with unfamiliar words. While readers review their lines, you may want to let the other students check out their books.

4. Once the students are familiar with their parts, have them line up in story order. Narrators should be on the audience's left in number order. Then Miss Lotta Scales, the principal and the children, with Molly last. Distribute the character signs. You should sit where you can prompt the readers if necessary.

5. Perform the script. After, ask the audience what they liked about how the actors read their lines. If time allows, let the audience have the parts and repeat the performance. The second time will be even better after students have seen how it can be done.

 **Book Exploring**

Go Exploring in Books *Reader's Theater Script*
www.lisablau.com/scripts/2001scripts/GoExploringinBooks.doc
Divide your class into four groups and have them read the script chorally, twice, to introduce the celebration.

 I Can Do It All At the Library

Read the brief book *I Can Do It All* by Mary E. Pearson (Scholastic Library Publishing, 2002) to the class. It lists 14 things a reader can do vicariously. Discuss with students other things they can do in the library, like research via the Internet, listen to a book on cassette, etc. Give each student a form that has 20 lines that all begin with "I can …" Set a timer and have students complete the sentences as many ways as they can. Give a special bookmark or allow an extra book at checkout for every student that comes up with more than 12, or a number you determine.

 Library Favorites

Duplicate a class set of the logic puzzle on page 73. Using the clues, have students place an "X" in the box when they determine that a person would not like that genre. Place a star if that is the correct genre. Once a star is determined, remember to "X" all other boxes in the star's row and column.

For a more kinesthetic experience that saves paper and toner, mount a class set of logic puzzles on construction paper and laminate. Give each student a sandwich bag with black and white beans. Have them use the black beans as the "yes" markers and the white as "no" markers. After you share the answers, students return the beans to their bag and the set is ready for the next class.

Answers:

Jason	suspense
Kaisa	mystery
Rachel	historical fiction
Lupe	science
Ian	poetry

 # Love Your Library

Post a question each day in your library, or ask it on the morning announcements. Have students enter their name and answer each day by grade level. I use small paper bags with grade level numbers on the front of each. Draw for winners at regular intervals. Award a free book, a bonus library pass, a Helper of the Day or other prize.

Sample Questions:

- How many months has the (your school name) library been open?

- How many books does our library have? Hint: It is more than ___ and less than ___.

- Name five nonfiction authors whose last name begins with the letter "J."

- Which book won the Caldecott Medal in 1981?

- Which were the Caldecott honor books in 1981?

- Name three books that have "green" in the title.

- How many shelves hold books in our library?

- How many videocassettes are available for teachers? Hint: More than ___, less than ___.

- What is a picture book that has won the Newbery Medal? What year did it win?

- Name two nonfiction books that have won the Newbery Medal.

- There are ___ weeks in our school year. If you checked out ___ books each week, how many could you have read by the end of the year?

- Name three authors who write a mystery series.

- How many different books does the library own by Chris Van Allsburg?

- What is the address of the library's Internet home page?

- Find out a favorite book of three teachers.

- Who invented the numbering system we use in our library and in what year?

- How many computers can be used by students in our library?

- Our librarian, _____, began her library work in _____. How many years has she been helping students in the library?

- How many student magazine subscriptions does the library receive? Name three of them.

- Name three reasons a library is a place to love.

 # Resources

Books:

Andrew Carnegie: Builder of Libraries by Charnan Simon. Scholastic Library Publishing, 1997. (3–5) Carnegie, an immigrant from Scotland, amassed a fortune worth $300 million that he spent on 8,000 church organs, research to cure diseases, construction of colleges, trade schools, a world-class art gallery, museum and concert hall. He is best known for the building of 2,811 libraries, including the one in *Goin' Someplace Special.* He left the Carnegie Corporation to continue giving away his wealth after his death.

> *There is not such a cradle of democracy upon the earth as the Free Public Library, this republic of letters, where neither rank, office, nor wealth receives the slightest consideration.* **–Andrew Carnegie**

Beverly Billingsly Borrows a Book by Alexander Stadler. Harcourt, 2002. (K–2) Beverly learns that not only does the library not charge a thousand dollars or put her in jail for an overdue book, as she had heard, but she discovers that she can make friends in the library. Compare with *The Librarian from the Black Lagoon* by Mike Thaler (Scholastic, 1997).

Book! Book! Book! by Deborah Bruss. Scholastic, 2000. (K–2) The animals pout and grow bored when the children return to school. They decide to visit the library to see if they can find something to do. Only the chicken is able to make the librarian understand what she wants.

Clarence the Copy Cat by Patricia Lakin. Random House, 2002. (K–2) Clarence is booted from one job to another because he is too kind to kill mice. He is adopted at the library and asked to rid it of one pesky mouse. Clarence's attempts to humanely remove the mouse are funny and principled.

A Day with a Librarian by Jan Kottke. Scholastic Library Publishing, 2000. (K–2) Small close-up photos illustrate Mrs. Napolitano's statements about what she does. Followed by a glossary, bibliography and index.

The Deserted Library Mystery created by Gertrude Chandler Warner. Albert Whitman, 1991. (3–5) The Alden children try to reorganize and prepare the boarded-up Rock Falls Library to qualify for landmark status. As they do, they befriend Miguel and discover that someone is trying to steal an old Civil War sword that is one of the artifacts in the library.

Down Cut Shin Creek: The Pack Horse Librarians of Kentucky by Kathi Appelt. HarperCollins, 2001. (4–5) From 1935 to 1943, intrepid women rode horses and mules into the mountains and hills of Kentucky to provide books and magazines to victims of the Great Depression. The book is generously illustrated with photographs and followed by a list of interviews, books and original source materials used in the writing. An index is also included.

D. W.'s Library Card by Marc Brown. Little, Brown and Company, 2001. (K–2) D. W. learns to write her name so she can get a library card, and is then burdened by the perceived responsibility of keeping the book in perfect condition.

Going to the Library by Melinda Radabaugh. Heinemann Library, 2002. (K–2) Numerous small pictures, large simple text and a picture glossary help students understand what to expect on a trip to a library. There is a simple quiz and index.

Goin' Someplace Special by Patricia McKissack. Simon & Schuster, 2001. (2–5) 'Tricia Ann persists despite the pain caused by numerous Jim Crow laws in her small town in order to go to the Carnegie library, which is open to all. Pair this with the Carnegie biography.

I Can Do It All by Mary E. Pearson. Scholastic Library Publishing, 2002. (K–1) This brief book begins, "I zoom in a plane. I sail on a ship." It concludes with "I visit the king. When I go to the library, I can do anything!"

The Inside-Outside Book of Libraries by Roxie Munro and Julie Cummins. Dutton, 1996. (3–5) Give older students a tour of the variety of libraries that serve people without charge. Large pictures describe 11 libraries, including the Folsom State Prison Library, The Berkeley (CA) Tool Lending Library and the library aboard the aircraft carrier *Abraham Lincoln.*

The Librarian from the Black Lagoon by Mike Thaler. Scholastic, 1997. (K–2) A young child hears horrors about the librarian, the school library and its policies. The reality is a comfort to the child and the reader.

Librarians by Dee Ready. Capstone Press, 1998. (1–3) Explains the jobs of a librarian, including library aides and the bookmobile. A bibliography, glossary and index are included.

The Library Dragon by Carmen Agra Deedy. Peachtree Publishers, 1994. (K–3) A library dragon is converted to a gentle librarian when a small child reads to her.

Library Lil by Suzanne Williams. Dial, 1997. (1–4) In this tall tale version, Lil converts a town of TV addicts to book lovers, including a tough motorcycle gang.

The Library of Congress by Allan Fowler. Scholastic Library Publishing, 1996. (2–5) To keep the young American Congress informed, John Adams signed a bill for $5,000 that purchased 152 books from England in 1801. This was the beginning of the Library of Congress. When most of the books were destroyed during the War of 1812, Congress purchased Thomas Jefferson's personal library (6,000 books). Abe Lincoln opened it to the public in 1864. Find out more in this interesting book about the national library.

Locked in the Library! by Marc Brown. Little, Brown and Company, 1998. (1–3) Arthur and Francine are accidentally locked in the public library.

Meg Mackintosh and the Mystery in the Locked Library: A Solve-It-Yourself Mystery by Lucinda Landon. Secret Passage Press, 1996. (2–4) Students can try to solve the mystery not only from the text, but also from the drawings, maps, illustrations and detailed notes taken by Meg in her notebook within the book. In this mystery, Meg is trying to discover how a rare book was stolen from a locked library.

Ms. Davison, Our Librarian by Alice Flanagan. Scholastic Library Publishing, 1996. (K–2) Though the language is simple, words few and font large, this book describes numerous things the public librarian does for her patrons.

Red Light, Green Light, Mama and Me by Cari Best. Orchard Books, 1995. (1–2) Lizzie accompanies her mother to work as the children's librarian at the public library. Because Lizzie participates in many of the tasks in the library, young students get a good feel for what librarians do.

Richard Wright and the Library Card by William Miller. Lee & Low Books, 1997. (2–5) Richard Wright, author of the international bestseller *Native Son,* was not allowed to borrow books from his Tennessee library because he was black. A white coworker lets Richard use his card as if he were borrowing books for the coworker. The library became the inspiration for his writing career and his passion for reading.

School Librarians by Cynthia Klingel and Robert B. Noyed. Rourke Press, 2001. (2–3) Focuses on the school librarian.

Stella Louella's Runaway Book by Lisa Campbell Ernst. Simon & Schuster, 1998. (2–3) Librarians and students alike can identify with the frantic search for a lost library book.

Tiny Goes to the Library by Cari Meister. Viking, 2000. (K–1) This easy reader has two to eight words per page. Tiny is a huge dog that can't go in the library while his master selects books. But he is read to as his reward for pulling the book-laden wagon home.

Tomás and the Library Lady by Pat Mora. Random House, 1997. (2–4) Inspired by the life of Tomás Rivera, a migrant worker's son who became chancellor of the University of California at Riverside. Students experience the life of a family that follows the crops. Tomás is encouraged to read and check out books by the librarian in one of the small towns near the fields. Compare this experience with that of Andrew Carnegie.

Web sites:

Carnegie for Kids
www.carnegie.org/sub/kids/libraries.html
Find out more about this Scottish immigrant who funded 2,509 libraries in the U.S., Scotland, Ireland, England, Australia and New Zealand. Click on seven links to Carnegie libraries in seven states and in Scotland, his birth country.

Go Exploring in Books *Reader's Theater Script*
www.lisablau.com/scripts/2001scripts/GoExploringinBooks.doc

IPL Kidspace
ipl.sils.umich.edu/div/kidspace
Includes lots of kid friendly sites on this "first public library of and for the Internet community" like Science Fair, Stately Knowledge, Story Hour, Ask a Question, POTUS and Culture Quest World Tour.

Kids Web: The Digital Library for K–12 Students
www.npac.syr.edu/textbook/kidsweb
Contains selected sites for students K–12 arranged by age level and subjects like Arts, Sciences, Social Studies and Miscellaneous (comics, games, movies, music and sports). Also includes a site for key pals, student home pages and e-mail directories.

Reader's Theater Script
The Library Dragon

Adapted from *The Library Dragon* by Carmen Agra Deedy.
Illustrated by Michael P. White. Peachtree Publishers, 1994.

Readers: Miss Lotta Scales; Albert Hoops; Child 1; Child 2; Principal; Miss Lemon; Molly Brickmeyer; Narrators 1–8

Narrator 1   Sunrise Elementary School had a **big** problem.

Narrator 2   The new librarian, Miss Lotta Scales, was a real dragon.

Narrator 3   Miss Lotta Scales was hired to guard the Library.

Narrator 4   And she took her job seriously.

Narrator 1   She kept a fiery eye out to make sure no one removed any books from the shelves.

Narrator 2   Her motto was, "A place for everything, and that's where it stays."

Narrator 3   The very thought of sticky little fingers pawing and clawing her precious books just made her hot under the collar.

Narrator 4   Miss Lotta Scales thought that the way some books spread a fear of dragons was positively **in-flam-ma-tor-y!**

Lotta Scales   Books that depict cruelty to dragons should never have been published in the first place.

Narrator 1   She got so fired up about those dragon books that she burned them up.

Narrator 2   She **in-cin-e-rated** them!

Albert Hoops   *(Whispering.)* Well, that settles it. Where there's smoke, there's fire. That Miss Scales is a real dragon, all right.

Child 1   Do we have to go to the library?

Child 2   I'm scared of that Miss Lotta Scales.

Narrator 3   It wasn't long before the teachers stopped sending the children to the library.

Albert Hoops	Ow, that librarian is a hothead!
Principal	Miss Scales, the children are complaining. Won't you try to cool down?
Lotta Scales	You want me to cool down? Well, that just burns me up!
Principal	Don't forget who does the hiring, Miss Scales.
Lotta Scales	Oh, really? And who does the firing?
Narrator 4	Miss Scales glared at him with such a hot look that the principal's tie caught on fire.
Principal	Now cut that out!
Lotta Scales	No smoking in the library.
Narrator 5	The principal fumed. The teachers were incensed.
Narrator 6	Worst of all, the children had missed reading and story time for weeks and their grades were going up in smoke.
Narrator 7	Sweet Miss Lemon, the kindergarten teacher, tried to reason with Miss Lotta Scales.
Miss Lemon	… and most importantly, Miss Scales, dear, the children miss story time.
Lotta Scales	Story time, schmorie-time! If I let these gooey snotty children touch the books, this library won't last a week.
Narrator 8	Miss Lotta Scales looked fiercely at Miss Lemon.
Narrator 5	But Miss Lemon was not afraid.
Miss Lemon	You know, Miss Scales, we all love the books as much as you do … but the library belongs to the children.
Narrator 6	Miss Lotta Scales huffed and she puffed and she blew some flames Miss Lemon's way.
Narrator 7	Miss Lemon rushed out of the library just ahead of the flames.
Narrator 8	Lotta Scales was getting burned out at her job.
Lotta Scales	*(Sadly.)* Being a Library Dragon can be such a lonely job.
Molly	Is anyone here? I can't see anything without my glasses.
Narrator 1	Molly bumped into a bookshelf because she could not see too well.

Narrator 2	A book fell onto her lap.
Narrator 3	Molly held it close to her face and began to read out loud.
Narrator 4	A class of second graders heard a story being read aloud, and they tiptoed into the library to listen.
Child 1	Could you speak up, please, Molly?
Child 2	Hey guys, listen to this. Someone is reading a story in the library.
Narrator 1	Word of story time in the library spread like wildfire at Sunrise Elementary School.
Narrator 2	Everyone was listening.
Narrator 3	Even the Library Dragon.
Narrator 4	And her ears were burning.
Molly	… I love you, Snuff.
Lotta Scales	Give me that book, Molly Brickmeyer!
Molly	Here you go, Miss Scales.
Narrator 5	Miss Lotta Scales sniffed the book.
Narrator 6	She checked the spine for cracks.
Narrator 7	She checked each page for stains and smudges.
Narrator 8	Finally Miss Scales cleared the smoke from her throat.
Lotta Scales	Now, where were we? Here it is … I love you, Snuff.
Narrator 5	The children were too nervous to listen.
Narrator 6	But when Molly Brickmeyer climbed up onto Miss Lotta Scales's lap …
Child 1	And didn't get scorched …
Child 2	They relaxed and began to enjoy the story.
Molly	You're warm.
Lotta Scales	Don't interrupt!
Narrator 7	Then the most amazing thing happened!
Narrator 8	Everyone was listening so intently that they almost missed it.

Narrator 1	As Miss Lotta Scales read, her scales began to fall on the floor …
Narrator 2	… with a clickety-clack, clickety-clack, clickety-clack.
Narrator 3	Until all that was left was Miss Lotty—
Narrator 4	—the librarian and storyteller, sitting on a mountain of yellow, green and purple scales.
Child 1	We all warmed up to Miss Lotty right away.
Child 2	Now we love Library Day.
Molly	Just remember, every librarian needs to be a little bit of a dragon—or else …
Lotta Scales	*(In a sweet voice.)* … who would guard the books?

The End

The Library Dragon Character Signs

Molly Brickmeyer

Miss Lemon

Miss Lotta Scales

Principal

Stretchy Library Lessons: Seasons & Celebrations

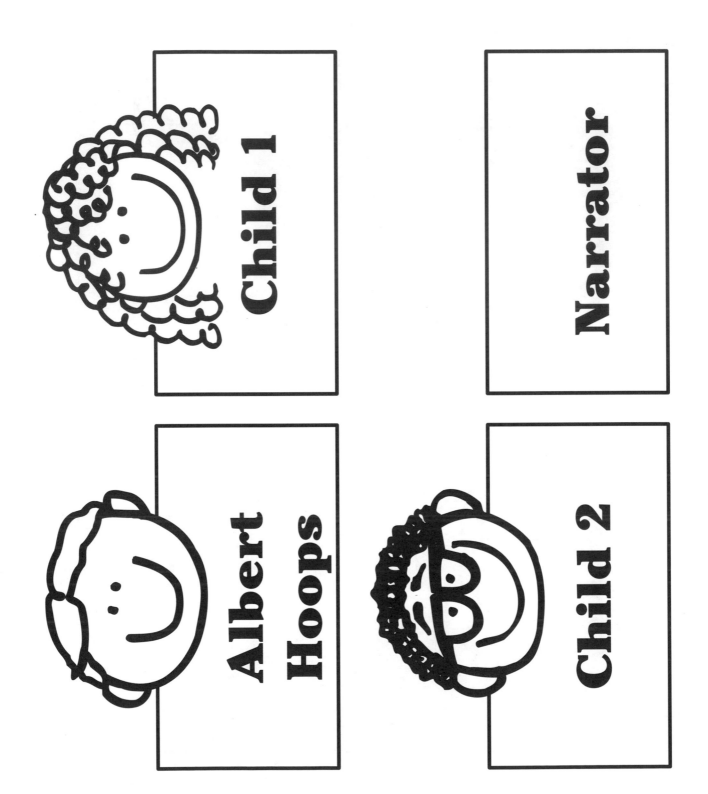

Library Favorites Logic Puzzle

Can you match each child to his or her favorite types of books? Place an "X" in the box when you determine that a person does not like that type of book. Place a star in the box for the correct type of book. Once a star is determined, "X" all of the boxes in the star's row and column.

	Poetry	Historical Fiction	Science	Mystery	Suspense
Jason					
Kaisa					
Rachel					
Lupe					
Ian					

Clues

1. Rachel and Lupe do not like scary stories.

2. Kaisa loves to use clues to solve the story.

3. Ian especially likes verse.

4. Lupe prefers nonfiction.

Stretchy Library Lessons: Seasons & Celebrations

Spring

Spring in the world!
And all things are made new!
–Richard Hovey

Spring Vegetables

Grades: K–3

Purposes:

- To learn about the vegetables that are planted in the spring.

- To learn which parts of a variety of plants are edible.

- To share a humorous story.

Format: Flannel Board Story, Sharing Realia *(optional)*, Compare/Contrast Main Characters, Group Response Activity

Materials:

- variety of vegetables, either the real things, papier-mâché or photographs

- flannel vegetables

- flannel board

- length of yarn that can be tied around the middle of the flannel board

- *Tops & Bottoms* by Janet Stevens (Harcourt, 1995)

- transparency of Tops, Bottoms or Middles? chart from page 80

- character dolls of Bear and Hare from Crocodile Creek *(optional)*

Prepare in Advance: Gather a variety of vegetables. These can be preprinted flannel or magnetic board figures, papier-mâché or the real thing. Divide your flannel board in half horizontally with a piece of yarn. Make a transparency of the Tops, Bottoms or Middles? chart.

Activity Directions:

1. Discuss the following questions with your students to prepare them for the activities:

   What are vegetables? They are the edible parts of soft-stemmed plants. Vegetables are grouped by the part of the plant they come from—leaves (lettuce, cabbage, brussels sprouts), stalks (celery, rhubarb), roots (carrot, parsnip), tubers (potato, yams), bulbs (onion, garlic) and flowers (broccoli, cauliflower). Tomatoes, which are the fruit of the plant, are often considered a vegetable.

   When are vegetables planted? When are they usually harvested? How many vegetables can be named?

   Can you tell how each of the edibles we named is grown? Does it come from a tree, a vine, a bush or a single plant?

   Does where you live influence what kinds of vegetables are available? Why or why not?

2. As you hold up each vegetable, or its picture, ask if the part we eat grows above or below the ground (bottoms). If it grows above, do we eat the leaves (tops) or the "fruit" (middles)?

3. Show the title page of *Tops & Bottoms,* where the book's gutter acts like the surface of the ground. Explain that in this book, the clever and hungry Hare tricks lazy Bear. Tell them to listen carefully to see if they can figure out the trick.

4. Share the book, then ask what the trick was.

5. Draw a Venn diagram to compare/contrast Bear and Hare.

6. Show the transparency. Complete with student help.

   Solution:

Food	Plant Part	Position
Celery	Stem	Middle
Rice	Seeds	Middle
Corn	Seeds	Middle
Potato	Root	Bottom
Broccoli	Flowers	Tops
Cauliflower	Flowers	Tops
Onion	Root	Bottom
Radish	Root	Bottom
Lettuce	Leaves	Tops
Spinach	Leaves	Tops
Rhubarb	Stem	Middle
Carrot	Root	Bottom

 # Measuring the Garden

In *A Harvest of Color,* Molly gives tips on measuring a garden using her body measurements instead of a ruler. For this activity, put children into groups of three and give them a fabric tape measure along with the chart on page 81. They should measure their bodies as listed by Molly and compare with their two friends. Have them prepare to discuss if these differences in measurements could cause a problem in a garden. Which measurement has the most difference between the three students? Why? Which has the least difference? Why?

 # "The Little Red Hen"

The story of the Little Red Hen helps students understand the events from wheat kernel to bread. Use *Stretchy Library Lessons: Reading Activities* by Pat Miller (Upstart Books, 2003) to retell the story in sign language to represent the cat, the dog, the duck and the Little Red Hen, as well as the major actions. You'll find the story and the hand signs along with storytelling sequence strips, and nine story cards for less able readers to put in order.

 # What's My Vegetable?

Divide the class into two teams. You will need a large drawing of a beanstalk (each leaf is a space for the game). Gather a variety of fruits and vegetables. You can use photographs, (the Freymann books like *How Are You Peeling? Foods with Moods* are fun), papier-mâché fruits and vegetables or the real thing.

Ask students to number their paper from 1 to __ depending on how many fruits and vegetables you have. Show each team a fruit or vegetable. As a team, they discuss and write the names as you show each one. For example, you may hold up a carrot, real, fake or photograph. Students discuss in their groups, then write down a team answer. When all have been written, begin the game by showing the team an item, say the seventh one. Then ask Team 1 what they wrote for number 7. If they are correct, move their marker up the beanstalk. The first team to get to the top wins an extra book to check out. An alternate way to play is to have all students complete their own list of fruits and vegetables as you display them. They can then share their answers when called upon in order to reach the top of the beanstalk.

 # The New Improved Fruit Game

The New Improved Fruit Game
www.2020tech.com/fruit/index.html
This game involves logical deduction and a mathematical strategy. The site explains the Quick Rules. The object of the game is to remove the last fruit from the table. Students play against the computer. The site includes directions for the mathematical strategy for winning. Older children can use the math strategy. Younger players will enjoy trial and error until they tire of being beaten by the computer.

 **Resources**

General Books:

Stretchy Library Lessons: Reading Activities by Pat Miller. UpstartBooks, 2003.

Books About Fruits and Vegetables:

An Alphabet Salad: Fruits and Vegetables from A to Z by Sarah L. Schuette. Capstone Press, 2003. (K–2) Each page shows the alphabet in upper- and lowercase with the letter of the edible highlighted. Half the page is a large close-up of the fruit or vegetable. The other half gives its name and some simple facts about it. End matter includes the list of edibles with two more facts about each, the food guide pyramid, a glossary, index and bibliography.

Brave Potatoes by Toby Speed. Putnam, 2000. (K–3) Potatoes visit the fair grounds after dark for an adventure, unaware that a wicked chef named Hackemup has other plans for them. This book is very funny while it addresses the fate of vegetables grown for food. Older students will enjoy the wordplay and puns.

Corn—On and Off the Cob by Allan Fowler. Scholastic Library Publishing, 1994. (K–2) What food is grown on more American farms than any other? Did you guess corn? However, farm animals eat most of that corn!

A Day in the Life of a Farmer by Heather Adamson. Capstone Press, 2004. (K–2) The book combines large photos with simple text to show the life of a farmer from 5 A.M. until he comes home for dinner at 6:30 P.M. Along the way, it answers questions children may have, like "Why are there so many buildings on a farm?" The book concludes with a labeled diagram of a tractor, glossary, index and resources for more information. For kindergartners, share *We Need Farmers* by Lola M. Schaefer (Capstone Press, 1999).

Eating Pairs: Counting Fruits and Vegetables by Twos by Sarah Schuette. Capstone Press, 2003. (K–2) Count from 2 to 20, and then skip to 100. Pages include a column of the numbers with the featured one highlighted. The fruits or vegetables are large and clear and include an interesting paragraph for each. For example, for eight: "Pears are related to apples and are part of the rose family. All types of pears are juicy and sweet." At the end, groups of vegetables are shown and children are asked, "How many?" and "How do they grow?" In 10 circles are photos of the item with a phrase telling if they grow on trees, bushes or close to the ground. There is a bibliography, index and glossary.

Farmers Market by Carmen Parks. Harcourt, 2003. (K–3) A girl and her parents spend the day at the farmers' market selling the vegetables they've grown.

A Harvest of Color: Growing a Vegetable Garden by Melanie Eclare. Ragged Bears, 2001. (2–5) Six children grow potatoes, carrots, radishes, zucchini and string beans. Each child has a photo-journal section, followed by a page of tips based on what they learned. "You have to be patient to grow potatoes. Sam grew three crops of radishes in the same amount of time it took my potatoes to grow. —Robert." For kindergartners, share *Fall Harvest* by Gail Saunders-Smith (Capstone Press, 1998).

How Are You Peeling? Foods with Moods by Saxton Freymann and Joost Elffers. Scholastic, 1999. (K–5) The authors use large close-up photos of fruits and vegetables to illustrate a variety of emotions.

It's a Fruit, It's a Vegetable, It's a Pumpkin by Allan Fowler. Scholastic Library Publishing, 1995. (K–2) Children learn about squash, watermelon, pumpkins and other plants that grow on a vine.

Jody's Beans by Malachy Doyle. Candlewick Press, 1999. (2–4) From spring planting to fall harvest and eating, Jody and her grandfather are involved with runner beans.

One Bean by Anne Rockwell. Walker and Company, 1998. (K–1) *One Bean* follows the planting and raising of beans, from "I had one bean. It was dry and smooth and hard" to "I picked a few pods and ate the beans that grew inside them. And they were very, very good!"

Tops & Bottoms by Janet Stevens. Harcourt, 1995. (K–5) Hare does all the work in order to use the lazy Bear's land to raise his veggies. He gives Bear his choice of whether he wants his half of the crop from the tops, the bottoms or the middle of the plant. Each time, wily hare ends up with all the edible parts. This Caldecott winner is written vertically, with the gutter often used to separate the above- and belowground scenes.

The Ugly Vegetables by Grace Lin. Charlesbridge Publishing, 1999. (2–4) All the neighbors plant beautiful flowers that outshine the ugly Chinese vegetables grown by a young girl's mother. But when they are harvested and cooked, all the neighbors beg to trade flowers for her delicious Ugly Vegetable Soup. Recipe and pronunciation of Chinese vegetables is appended.

Nonfiction Books About Spring:

The Nature and Science of Rain by Jane Burton and Kim Taylor. Gareth Stevens, 1997. (3–5)

The Nature and Science of Spring by Jane Burton and Kim Taylor. Gareth Stevens, 1999. (3–5)

A Rainy Day by Lola M. Schaefer. Capstone Press, 1999. (K–1)

The Reasons for the Seasons by Gail Gibbons. Holiday House, 1995. (2–4)

Splish, Splash, Spring by Jan Carr. Holiday House, 2001. (K–2)

Spring by Terri DeGezelle. Capstone Press, 2002. (K–2)

Spring by Cynthia Klingel and Robert B. Noyed. Child's World, 2000. (1–3)

Spring by Gail Saunders-Smith. Capstone Press, 1998. (K–1)

Spring by Darlene Stille. Compass Point Books, 2001. (1–3)

Spring: An Alphabet Acrostic by Steven Schnur. Clarion Books, 1999. (2–5) Acrostic poetry that captures the sights, sounds and smells of spring.

Spring: Signs of the Season Around North America by Valerie J. Gerard. Picture Window Books, 2002. (K–3)

A Windy Day by Lola M. Schaefer. Capstone Press, 1999. (K–1)

Web sites:

Dole 5 A Day Fruits and Vegetables

www.dole5aday.com/Kids/K_Index.jsp

Click on pictures of 43 fruits and vegetables to find out how they help your body. There are also numerous fun and interesting games on this site.

Kids Ag Page

www.agr.state.il.us/kidspage/index.html

Pages include: On the Farm: Plants, Animals and More; From the Farm: Food and Other Things You Use Every Day; From Farm to Table: The Story of Milk; Farm Animals and Their Babies; Scrambled Word Match-Up; and Hidden Word Search.

The New Improved Fruit Game

www.2020tech.com/fruit/index.html

Spring Crafts

www.enchantedlearning.com/crafts/spring

Children can make all kinds of spring crafts at home or in the classroom, including greeting cards, flower crowns and eggshell plant pots.

Spring Online Games

www.kidsdomain.com/games/spring.html

Play 10 games to celebrate the coming of more daylight, including Math Baseball, Make a Butterfly and Get Dirty with Freddie the 4-Wheeler.

What Grows?

www.kidsfarm.com/crops.htm

Click on one of five fruits, hay, asparagus, wild flowers or farmer's market to see photos showing the crops growing and being harvested and sold.

Tops, Bottoms or Middles?

Food	Plant Part	Position
Celery		
Rice		
Corn		
Potato		
Broccoli		
Cauliflower		
Onion		
Radish		
Lettuce		
Spinach		
Rhubarb		
Carrot		

Measuring the Garden

Complete the chart. Measurements are from page 7 in *A Harvest of Color*.

Measurement	Me	Friend 1	Friend 2
Distance across one finger.			
Distance across two fingers.			
Distance from the tip of my index finger to my wrist.			
The length of my foot.			
The width of my hand with my thumb and fingers spread out.			
The length of my arm.			
The length of my thumbnail.			

Humor Month

Laughter is the shortest distance between two people.
–Victor Borge

Humor  MAIN ACTIVITY

Grades: 3–5 (Younger students will enjoy hearing many of the stories and briefly comparing them to the originals.)

Purposes:

- To analyze retellings and adaptations of traditional folk and fairy tales.

- To compare/contrast two or more versions and record findings.

Format: Read Aloud, Group Discussion, Small Group Participation.

Materials:

- copies of books listed in resources to make comparisons

- transparency of Adaptation Characteristics sheet from page 92

- transparency pen

- copies of Adaptation Characteristics sheet for each small group or pair

- words with definitions, written on chalkboard or on magnetic cards

Prepare in Advance: Pull or borrow as many titles as possible from the resources list. Group them together, perhaps with a tent card naming the original tale. In addition to the books on the list, have at least one copy of the original tale. Duplicate Adaptation Characteristics sheet and make a transparency. Set up the overhead projector and find water-based pen.

Activity Directions:

1. Explain to the students that we are going to share a variety of humorous books. They are written to be funny using a variety of techniques. Show them a copy of Grimm's Cinderella. Then show a variant from another culture. Explain the difference between an adaptation and a variant. An adaptation is a story based on a traditional one in which

at least three major changes have been made. They have a named author and do not come from the tradition of passing a story orally. A variant or retelling is one in which minor changes have been made in the story because of retellings by many tellers in many cultures. They are a result of many people telling the same story over time.

2. The following terms are the types of humor used in "fractured fairy tales." Discuss the terms and their definitions with your students.

   irony—1. the use of words that mean the opposite of what one really intends 2. a big difference between an actual and an expected result of a sequence of events

   parody—a written or musical work in which the style of an author or work is imitated for comic effect

   satire—something meant to make fun of and show the weaknesses of human nature or a particular person

   take-off—to mimic (to imitate closely or to make fun of by imitating)

   tongue-in-cheek—written or said to be humorous or ironic but not to be taken seriously

   (Definitions are from: *Word Central's Student Dictionary*. www.wordcentral.com. Merriam Webster Inc., 1998, 1999.)

3. The stories we will be examining today are not variants, but are deliberate adaptations in which the author has made major changes in the basic story. As we share the original and its adaptations, we will be looking or listening for the following changes:

   • change in role(s)

   • change in point of view

   • change in setting or time

   • addition or subtraction of major characters

   • change in the problem to be solved

   • change in the ending, more realistic

   • change in characters

   • other

4. Read the original to the students and talk about the characters, setting, time, problem and conclusion.

5. Then read adaptations as time allows. Keep the discussion light. Mention what the illustrator contributed to the humor and perhaps to a storyline not mentioned in the text. After each story, complete the chart, either as a class using the transparency or as groups completing the worksheet.

6. Share findings with the class if done in groups.

7. This lesson can be repeated throughout the month or year, using a different group of tales and their variants.

Shadow Stage

Materials:

- picture stretcher frame, at least 25" x 36"

- 1 yard of 45" opaque white fabric (thickness of a bed sheet)

- 2 dozen flat-head thumbtacks or staple gun

- 4 bookends

- Tacky glue

- 3½ yards of glittery trim

- 2 clip-on lights

- surge suppressor type extension cord in which to plug the lights and tape recorder

Directions:

1. Assemble stretcher frame.

2. Cut fabric 1½" wider than frame measurement on all four sides.

3. Spread fabric on flat surface. Center the stretcher frame on top of the fabric.

4. Begin at the edge. Fold the edge of the fabric under so it won't ravel, then fold it to the back edge of the frame and staple or tack at 2" intervals. Be sure there is a tack close to both ends. Tacks and staples will not pierce the slotted ends, so put one as close to them as you can.

5. Stand frame up, sandwiched between the bookends.

6. Clip the lights on the back of the frame so they face the fabric. Plug them into the extension cord.

7. Plug in the tape recorder. You are now ready to perform your pre-recorded story.

 ## Silly Parodies

Share the poetry set to familiar songs in the two books by Alan Katz, *Take Me Out of the Bathtub and Other Silly Dilly Songs* (Simon & Schuster, 2001) and *I'm Still Here in the Bathtub: Brand New Silly Dilly Songs* (Simon & Schuster, 2003).

 ## *No Bath Tonight* and *Double Trouble*

Share the fun of a humorous story by having your students act out one of these book related adaptations.

No Bath Tonight *Reader's Theater Script*

hometown.aol.com/rcswallow/NoBathTonight.html

A very active and dirty little boy doesn't want to take a bath until his Grandmother shows him how to make Little Boy Tea so she can read the "leaves." The script has four readers. (**Note:** There are some errors that should be corrected before making copies for students.)

Double Trouble in Walla Walla *Reader's Theater Script*

www.readinglady.com/Readers_Theater/Scripts/doubletrouble.doc

Older readers will enjoy the wordplay in the hilarious adaptation of *Double Trouble in Walla Walla* by Andrew Clements. For seven readers.

Humor Concentration

Use the Shower Curtain Jeopardy Board from page 39 as a Concentration Game for the whole class.

In a large font, write a riddle on each of a dozen cards or more. Write the answer on a dozen other cards. Mix them up and put them in the pockets face down. Put a transparency with a very large number in the front of each pocket, so students can ask for card number 8, for example.

Or you may want to make a transparency that shows all the answers and then ask students the riddles, one by one. They can look at the answers on the transparency and guess which is correct.

Following are some riddles from the Read-it! Joke Books series by Michael Dahl (Picture Window Books, 2003).

- **Animal Quack-Ups**

  How can you tell that elephants like to swim? *They always have their trunks on.*

  What's the worst thing about being an octopus? *Washing your hands before dinner.*

  Why did the chicken cross the playground? *To get to the other slide.*

- **Bell Buzzers**

  Knock knock. *Who's there?* Howie. *Howie who?* I'm fine, thanks. How are you?

- **Monster Laughs**

  What kind of music do mummies like? *Wrap.*

  Why doesn't the vampire have many friends? *Because he's a pain in the neck.*

  What does the Cyclops eat for dessert? *Eyes cream.*

- **School Daze**

  Why was Cinderella thrown off the school's soccer team? *She ran away from the ball.*

  In what school do you have to drop out to graduate? *Skydiving school.*

- **Who's There?**

  Knock knock. *Who's there?* Cows go. *Cows go who?* No, cows go, "Moo."

  Knock knock. *Who's there?* Boo. *Boo who?* Why are you crying?

- **Zoodles**

  What kind of dog has no tail, no nose, and no fur? *A hot dog.*

  Who steals soap from the bathroom? *The robber duckie!*

 # Become a Cartoonist

Cartoon Classroom: Brick by Brick
library.thinkquest.org/3538
A team of five fifth graders from Massachusetts developed this site as their ThinkQuest entry. Students can meet six cartoonists, including Bil Keane *(Family Circus),* Charles Schulz *(Peanuts)* and Jim Davis *(Garfield).* Subsequent sites include an explanation of nine types of humor and a humor challenge, and how to become a cartoonist with three practice situations online.

 # Resources

General Humor Books:

Double Trouble in Walla Walla by Andrew Clements. Millbrook Press, 1997. (2–5)

I'm Still Here in the Bathtub: Brand New Silly Dilly Songs by Alan Katz. Simon & Schuster, 2003. (2–5)

No Bath Tonight by Jane Yolen. HarperCollins, 1978. (K–2)

Read-it! Joke Books series by Michael Dahl. Picture Window Books, 2003. (K–3)

Take Me Out of the Bathtub and Other Silly Dilly Songs by Alan Katz. Simon & Schuster, 2001. (2–5)

The Boy Who Cried Wolf Books:

Betsy Who Cried Wolf by Gail Carson Levine. HarperCollins, 2002. (2–5) Sarcastic, silly sheep add to the humor of this story of a girl who is conscientious about her job but is constantly undermined by a wily wolf.

The Wolf Who Cried Boy by Bob Hartman. Putnam, 2002. (2–5) Little Wolf is tired of his mother's cooking and wants to eat a real boy. In his eagerness to find one, he "cries boy" too often, so his parents stop believing him, even when a troop of Boy Scouts marches through their living room.

Cinderella Books:

Bubba the Cowboy Prince: A Fractured Texas Tale by Helen Ketteman. Scholastic, 1997. (2–5) This Texas version features Bubba and his wicked stepbrothers. He is assisted by a fairy godcow. The dialogue will have even a Bronx native sounding like a Texan, and illustrator James Warhola exaggerates the humor.

Cinderella's Rat by Susan Meddaugh. Houghton Mifflin, 1997. (2–4) Learn the never before revealed details of that magic night from Cinderella's rat turned coachman.

Cinderella Skeleton by Robert D. San Souci. Harcourt, 2000. (3–5) This is a funny/scary version featuring skeletons that have some difficulties finding romance and a normal life.

Cinder-Elly by Frances Minters. Viking, 1994. (2–4) This updated parody has Cinder-Elly going to a basketball game in glass sneakers.

Ella Enchanted by Gail Carson Levine. HarperCollins, 1997. (4–5) It's not until one is well into the plot that she realizes that Ella, cursed at birth by a well-meaning fairy that wishes her to be obedient, is a fully realized Cinderella character. But this Ella is spirited, smart and not happy with her fate.

Fanny's Dream by Caralyn and Mark Buehner. Dial, 1996. (2–5) Fanny waits for her fairy godmother to make her wishes come true, but Heber Jensen, a farmer, shows up instead. He gives her no riches, but does give her lots of love and three children. When her tardy fairy godmother finally shows up, Fanny declines her offer.

Joe Cinders by Marianne Mitchell. Henry Holt and Company, 2002. (K–3) In this Southwest version, Joe manages to get to the fiesta to win the hand of Miss Rosalinda.

The Emperor's New Clothes Books:

The Dinosaur's New Clothes: A Retelling of the Hans Christian Andersen Tale by Diane Goode. Blue Sky Press, 1999. (2–5) This dinosaur makeover of the famous swindle is set in the Palace of Versailles during the lush styles of Louis XIV. The illustrations add as much humor as the text.

The Emperor's Old Clothes by Kathryn Lasky. Harcourt, 1999. (2–5) An old farmer finds the emperor's discarded clothes. He wears them to the parade and is astonished to see the emperor naked. When he gets home, he finds his tasks impossible in the oversized clothing, and when chick bursts into laughter, the farmer realizes how foolish he looks.

The Principal's New Clothes by Stephanie Calmenson. Scholastic, 1991. (2–5) This time a vain principal is embarrassed in front of his students when he falls for the tailor's story about clothes that will help him evaluate his staff.

The Frog Prince Books:

The Frog and the Princess and the Prince and the Mole and the Frog and the Mole and the Princess ... by John Bear. Ten Speed Press, 1994. (K–3) This reversible book has the frog turning into a prince when kissed, but the princess becomes a mole! With each kiss, the one being kissed becomes royal; the one kissing becomes an animal.

The Frog Prince—Continued by Jon Scieszka. Viking, 1991. (2–5) Scieszka explains what happens after the "happily ever after."

The Horned Toad Prince by Jackie Mims Hopkins. Peachtree Publishers, 2000. (2–5) In this Southwest version, Reba Jo is unhappy about having to keep her promise to a very persistent horned toad. The surprise ending makes an excellent opportunity for students to write what they think happens next.

Pondlarker by Fred Gwynne. Simon & Schuster, 1990. (3–5) Frog Pondlarker searches for the princess to turn him into a prince. When he finds one who has kissed millions of frogs and still hasn't found a prince to suit her, he decides that a frog is a fine thing to be.

Hansel and Gretel Books:

The Diary of Hansel and Gretel by Kees Moerbeek. Simon & Schuster, 2002. (2–5) To learn the true story of Hansel and Gretel, read Gretel's diary, complete with her drawings and notes, and a newspaper article purportedly by the Brothers Grimm. It includes a pop-up gingerbread house.

Dom DeLuise's Hansel and Gretel by Dom DeLuise. Simon & Schuster, 1997. (2–5) This is the health-conscious version of two children who try to escape from Glut Annie Sag and return to their father and his health food store.

'T Pousette et 't Poulette: A Cajun Hansel and Gretel by Sheila Hebert Collins. Pelican Publishing Company, 2001. (3–5) The dialect will take one to the Cajun swamps where Hansel and Gretel seek to escape from the wicked woman who wants to eat them.

Jack and the Beanstalk Books:

The Giant's Toe by Brock Cole. Farrar, Straus and Giroux, 1986. (2–5) This is the prequel that explains Jack and the giant's relationship.

Jack and the Beanstalk by Steven Kellogg. William Morrow & Co., 1991. (2–5) The plot is traditional, but the actions that show in the illustrations definitely are not.

Jack and the Giant: A Story Full of Beans by Jim Harris. Northland Publishing AZ, 1997. (K–3) In this version, Jack climbs the beanstalk to outsmart Wild Bill Hiccup, the cattle rustler.

Jim and the Beanstalk by Raymond Briggs. Putnam, 1989. (3–5) Jack's son visits an aging giant and gives him considerable help.

Kate and the Beanstalk by Mary Pope Osborne. Simon & Schuster, 2000. (2–5) Kate climbs the beanstalk to retrieve the items stolen from her father, to avenge his death and to make her mother rich.

Look Out, Jack! The Giant is Back! by Tom Birdseye. Holiday House, 2001. (2–5) In this sequel, the giant's brother comes after Jack. Compare this version with *Kate and the Beanstalk*.

The Little Red Hen Books:

Cook-a-Doodle-Doo by Susan Stevens Crummel. Harcourt, 1999. (K–3) A young rooster, descendant of the Little Red Hen, finds he has too much help from his friends Pig, Turtle and Iguana as he struggles to make Strawberry Shortcake. Recipe included.

The Little Red Hen Makes a Pizza by Philemon Sturges. Dutton, 1999. (1–4) The Little Red Hen meets with the same lack of success when she wants to make a pizza.

Mr. Wolf's Pancakes by Jan Fearnley. M E Media LLC, 2001. (K–3) The townspeople rudely refuse to help Mr. Wolf make pancakes until they smell them cooking.

Little Red Riding Hood Books:

Bridget and the Gray Wolves by Pija Lindenbaum. R & S Books, 2001. (2–5) This Swedish version is full of slapstick as Bridget, lost from her day-care field trip, encounters a group of dim-witted wolves.

Little Red Cowboy Hat by Susan Lowell. Henry Holt and Company, 1997. (2–4) No huntsman is needed to rescue spunky Grandma and the hard-to-fool Little Red Cowboy Hat.

Little Red Riding Hood: A Newfangled Prairie Tale by Lisa Campbell Ernst. Simon & Schuster, 1995. (K–3) In this prairie version, Little Red has a spunky grandmother to help with the hapless wolf.

Little Red Ronnika by Bobby Jackson. Multicultural Publications, 1999. (3–5) Little Red Ronnika encounters a crafty, rapping wolf in this African-American version.

Little Red Snapperhood: A Fishy Fairy Tale by Neal Gilbertsen. Graphic Arts Center Publishing Co., 2003. (K–3) A little fish meets a wolf eel as she carries a baked octopi to her grandmother's house.

No Dinner! The Story of the Old Woman and the Pumpkin by Jessica Souhami. Marshall Cavendish, 2000. (2-5) This Southeast Asian folktale will remind students of the Red Riding Hood story as an old woman is accosted by a wolf as she tries to cross the forest to visit her granddaughter.

Petite Rouge: A Cajun Red Riding Hood by Mike Artell. Dial, 2001. (3–5) Another Cajun variant, this one includes a brief Cajun history and helpful glossary. Petite Rouge, a goose, encounters Claude, an old gator who tries to prevent her from visiting her Grandmére.

The Princess and the Pea Books:

The Cowboy and the Black-eyed Pea by Tony Johnston. Putnam, 1992. (2–5) Wealthy Farethee Well is looking for a sensitive mate. To test for a true cowboy she places a black-eyed pea beneath the saddle blanket of each suitor and sends him off to ride the range. When one discomforted cowboy asks for more and more padding, Farethee knows she has found her man.

The Princess and the Pizza by Mary Jane Auch. Holiday House, 2002. (2–5) Princess Paulina competes against two other princesses to win the hand of Prince Rupert. She knows the trick of the pea, but claims it is "so once-upon-a-time." Instead, she uses her cooking talents to best the princess with a very long braid and the one accompanied by seven little men.

The Very Smart Pea and the Princess-to-Be by Mini Grey. Random House, 2003. (2–5) This British author revisits the story from the pea's point of view.

Snow White Books:

The Seven Dwarfs by Etienne Delessert. Creative Company, 2001. (3–5) This sequel relates what happens after Snow White marries the prince and invites the seven dwarves to live in the palace with them.

Snow White in New York by Fiona French. Oxford University Press, 1990. (3–5) Snow White has been updated to New York in the 1920s. Now she is a flapper guarded by seven jazzmen.

Stone Soup Books:

Beware of Boys by Tony Blundell. Greenwillow Books, 1992. (2–5) Unfortunately, the wolf plans to make boy soup, but he chooses the wrong little boy to make it from.

Bone Button Borscht by Aubrey Davis. Kids Can Press, 1997. (2–4) A stranger convinces the stingy villagers that he can make borscht from buttons.

Stone Soup by Tony Ross. Puffin, 1991. (2–5) The soup maker is the Little Red Hen. The villainous Big Bad Wolf is tricked into not eating Hen when she tasks him to exhaustion while making stone soup.

The Three Bears Books:

Deep in the Forest by Brinton Turkle. Puffin, 1992. (K–2) In this wordless book, Baby Bear visits Goldilocks house in her absence, with the same distressing results.

Dusty Locks and the Three Bears by Susan Lowell. Henry Holt and Company, 2001. (K–3) Children will enjoy this Western style Goldilocks story.

Goldie and the Three Bears by Diane Stanley. HarperCollins, 2003. (K–3) Goldie's search for a friend who is "just right" takes her to the home of the three bears.

Goldilocks & the Three Bears by Tony Ross. Overlook, 1992. (2–5) This is the modern version complete with color television and the same negative reaction to the bad-mannered Goldilocks.

Goldilocks Returns by Lisa Campbell Ernst. Simon & Schuster, 2000. (K–3) Fifty years later, Goldilocks returns to make amends to the Three Bears.

Gordon Loggins and the Three Bears by Linda Bailey. Kids Can Press, 1997. (K–3) Gordon Loggins enters a secret doorway in the library. He emerges into the midst of the Goldilocks story, where he is the main character.

Leola and the Honeybears: An African-American Retelling of Goldilocks and the Three Bears by Melodye Benson Rosales. Scholastic, 1999. (1–4) Leola remembers her manners too late, but her tears of contrition move Mama Bear, who sends Leola home to her Mama with a blackbird escort.

Mr. Wolf and the Three Bears by Jan Fearnley. Harcourt, 2002. (1–3) In this version from Great Britain, Goldilocks crashes the birthday party that Mr. Wolf has carefully planned and prepared. Baby Bear's clever grandmother solves the problem of the obnoxious guest. Recipes are included.

Rolling Along with Goldilocks and the Three Bears by Cindy Meyers. Woodbine House, 1999. (K–3) Baby Bear has a wheelchair and electric bed and takes therapy lessons at The Treetop Center. Goldilocks becomes fascinated with his adaptive equipment and the two become friends.

Tackylocks and the Three Bears by Helen Lester. Houghton Mifflin, 2002. (K–2) Beloved Tacky the Penguin and his friends act out the traditional story, with hilarious results.

Three Billy Goats Gruff Books:

The Three Armadillies Tuff by Jackie Mims Hopkins. Peachtree Publishers, 2002. (K–3) Three armadillo sisters plan to visit the Stomp and Chomp for some dancing, but are hindered from getting through the culvert by a mangy coyote. See *Stretchy Library Lessons: Reading Activities* by Pat Miller (UpstartBooks, 2003) for a Reader's Theater script and character masks for each reader.

Three Cool Kids by Rebecca Emberley. Little, Brown and Company, 1995. (2–5) Three goat kids live in a barren lot. They want to cross to the grassy lot across the grate, but a fierce rat blocks their way.

The Three Silly Girls Grubb by John and Ann Hassett. Houghton Mifflin, 2002. (2–5) Three little girls have to deal with a mean bully that lives under the bridge that crosses their route to the school bus. The eldest bests him by threatening to kiss him!

The Toll-Bridge Troll by Patricia R. Wolff. Harcourt, 1995. (3–5) Trigg must pass under a bridge on his way to school. He uses riddles to outwit the troll who demands a toll.

The Three Little Pigs Books:

Porkenstein by Kathryn Lasky. Blue Sky Press, 2002. (K–3) In this sequel, the brick house pig, Dr. Smart Pig, misses his two brothers, so he tries to construct a friend with disastrously funny results.

The Three Little Hawaiian Pigs and the Magic Shark by Donivee Martin Laird. Barnaby Books, 1994. (1–3) In this unique adaptation, the pigs live in houses made of pili grass, driftwood and lava rock. Their nemesis is an angry shark in disguise.

Three Little Javelinas by Susan Lowell. Northland Publishing AZ, 1992. (2–4) This Southwestern version explains why coyotes howl.

The Three Little Wolves and the Big Bad Pig by Eugene Trivizas. Simon & Schuster, 1993. (K–3) This time it's a pig hassling three little wolves with a surprise ending.

Three Pigs, One Wolf and Seven Magic Shapes by Grace Maccarone. Scholastic, 1997. (K–2) This Hello Math Reader incorporates magic shapes (tangrams), which the pigs use throughout the story.

The True Story of the 3 Little Pigs by Jon Scieszka. Viking, 1989. (3–5) The Wolf explains that the whole story is a misunderstanding that began with his cold and the need to borrow a cup of sugar.

Wait! No Paint! by Bruce Whatley. HarperCollins, 2001. (K–5) In this fresh and funny version, the illustrator runs out of red paint and causes havoc for the pigs, which appear green or pale because of lack of paint. The Voice is the illustrator talking with the pigs, who want to quit the story because they can't have a fire to keep the wolf out of the chimney.

Where's the Big Bad Wolf? by Eileen Christelow. Clarion Books, 2002. (K–3) A dumb dog detective tries to protect the three little pigs when their houses are blown down. The Big Bad Wolf has an alibi, but children will quickly catch on to the not so innocent "sheep" Esmeralda who is always on the scene and gives out bad, and comical, advice.

Web sites:

Cartoon Classroom: Brick by Brick
library.thinkquest.org/3538

Double Trouble in Walla Walla *Reader's Theater Script*
www.readinglady.com/Readers_Theater/Scripts/doubletrouble.doc

The Jokester
www.thejokester.net

No Bath Tonight *Reader's Theater Script*
hometown.aol.com/rcswallow/NoBathTonight.html

10 Reasons a Dog Shouldn't Use a Computer
merel.us/Joker/AnimalFrame.htm

Word Central's Student Dictionary
www.wordcentral.com

Adaptation Characteristics

Names: _____

Title	Changes were made to ...								
	type of characters	role of characters	point of view	setting	time	main characters were added or subtracted	main problem	ending	other (explain)

Pets Month

Whoever said you can't buy happiness forgot about puppies.
–Gene Hill

Celebrating the Working Dog

Grades: 3–5

Purpose:

• To learn about dogs who help humans.

Format: Read Aloud, Compare/Contrast Worksheets, Participatory Bulletin Board

Materials:

• copies of the parent letter from page 102 for each interested child

• bulletin board with caption "Four Legged Best Friends"

• a selection of books from the list below or others in your collection

Prepare in Advance: Mark passages or photographs to show students. In *My Life in Dog Years* by Gary Paulsen (Bantam Doubleday Dell, 1998), a good read aloud is the chapter called "Cookie" in which Gary Paulsen's dog saves him when he goes through the ice. Mark selections from numerous books to show students all the ways dogs are helpful to people. Duplicate parent letters. Put up bulletin board.

Activity Directions:

1. Use information from book selections to talk to students about the roles of guide dogs, service dogs and assistance dogs. Show them how dogs work as sheep and cattle herders, assistants for disabled children and adults, police protectors and "detectives" and, of course, as family members called pets. See resource list on pages 98–100.

2. Share excerpts from the books that talk about specific dogs and their roles. For remarkable feats by eight ordinary pets, share Peg Kehret's book *Shelter Dogs: Amazing Stories of Adopted Strays.*

3. As time allows, have students briefly share stories about their own pets.

4. Invite students to bring pictures of their dogs, cats and other pets. Use the letter on page 102 to request them. Display them on a bulletin board with the title: "Four-Legged Best Friends."

Selecting a Pet

Grades: K–2

Purposes:

- To weigh variables in choosing a dog.

- To read of the experiences of others in selecting a dog.

Format: Read Aloud, Group Participation

Materials:

- books about dog selection

    "Let's Get a Pup" Said Kate by Bob Graham (Candlewick Press, 2001)

    The Perfect Puppy for Me! by Jane O'Connor and Jessie Hartland (Viking, 2003)

    A Pup Just for Me; A Boy Just for Me by Dorothea Seeber (Philomel Books, 2000)

- copies of the parent letter from page 102 for each interested child

- bulletin board with caption "Four-Legged Best Friends"

- white board, chart tablet or chalkboard

Prepare in Advance: Gather books, duplicate parent letter and put up bulletin board.

Activity Directions:

1. Ask students how many of them have adopted a pet. Have them name important considerations when choosing a pet. List them on the board.

2. Share books on pet selection with students.

3. Read aloud one of the books to the class and discuss.

4. Invite students to bring pictures of their pet cat, dog, guinea pig, etc., for the bulletin board display. Review the guidelines for photos from the letter, and distribute copies. Remind them of the deadline for photo submissions and answer student questions.

Automotive Flannel/ Magnetic Board

Materials:

- large metal automotive drip pan

- 1" foam paintbrush

- 1 yard of 60" black felt

- Tacky glue

- black spray paint, matte finish

- 4½ yards of glittery trim

- clothespins to hold trim while glue dries

Directions:

1. Trace the flat side of the drip pan onto newspaper to make a pattern. Use the pattern to cut out the felt.

2. Spray the flat bottom of the drip pan. A dark background will make it easier for your students to see the story figures. The curved side will be the flannel board.

3. Generously apply the glue to the curved side of the pan using the foam brush.

4. Attach and smooth the pre-cut black felt. Do not stretch. Allow to dry.

5. Run a thick line of glue around the inside edge of the drip pan. Beginning at the top left corner, attach the trim, pressing it firmly into place and allowing a little extra in the curves of the pan.

6. If desired, use clothespins to hold the trim in place while drying.

Note: When making props to attach to the board, attach small bits of magnetic tape or small pieces of adhesive hook-and-loop tape. Attach the grabby end of the tape to the figure. The bigger the bits of tape, the harder it is on your flannel board.

Doggie Dictionary

Compile a list of words as defined by the family pet to make a Kitty or Doggie Dictionary. For example:

- **water dish**—a miniature swimming pool for the nose. While you drink, be sure to splash as much of the water out of the bowl as possible.

Trilingual B.I.N.G.O.

Make a set of flannel or magnetic board letters from the patterns on page 101 by tracing them onto felt or fun foam. Add a piece of hook and loop tape or a small magnet to each. Use them to teach the words to a familiar song in Spanish and French.

English "Bingo"

There was a farmer,
Who had a dog.
And Bingo was his name, OH!
B-I-N-G-O *(Repeat these letters twice more.)*
And Bingo was his name, OH!

Spanish "Bingo"

Hay un ranchero,
Que tiene un perro.
Y se llama Bingo, OH!
B *(beh)*, I *(ee)*, N *(en-ay)*, G *(hay)*, O *(oh)* *(Repeat these letters twice more.)*
Y se llama Bingo, OH!

French "Bingo"

Il y a un fermier,
Qui a un chien.
Et il s'appelle Bingo, OH!
B *(beh)*, I *(ee)*, N *(en)*, G *(jay)*, O *(oh)* *(Repeat these letters twice more.)*
Et il s'appelle Bingo, OH!

Note: After singing through once, repeat rhyme five more times. Each round, leave off an additional letter, beginning with B. Clap in its place, until with the last round, you are rhythmically clapping all five letters.

 # Drama for Dogs

Laura Kump, a reading specialist from Staten Island, New York, adapted the following scripts about three funny dogs. Go to her site, **www.readinglady.com,** for many more scripts.

Dog Breath: The Horrible Trouble with Hally Tosis *Reader's Theater Script*
www.readinglady.com/Readers_Theater/Scripts/dogbreath.doc
This script has ten parts.

Doris: A Dog's Life *Reader's Theater Script*
www.readinglady.com/Readers_Theater/Scripts/adogslife.doc
The script from *Yo Aesop! Get a Load of These Fables* by Paul Rosenthal has six parts.

The Hallo-Wiener *Reader's Theater Script*
www.readinglady.com/Readers_Theater/Scripts/hallowiener.doc
This script has 12 parts.

The Dog Show

Duplicate a class set of the logic puzzle from page 103. Using the clues, have students place a star in the box when they determine the dog, its name or its place. Place an "X" in the square if it is determined the owner does not have that dog, etc. Once a star is determined, remember to "X" all other boxes in the star's row and column.

For a more kinesthetic experience that saves paper and toner, mount a class set of logic puzzles on construction paper and laminate. Give each student a sandwich bag with black and white beans. Have them use the black beans as the "yes" markers and the white as "no" markers. After you share the answers, students return the beans to their bag and the set is ready for the next class.

Answers:

Sarah	first place, beagle, Tagalong
Joey	third place, collie, Snappy Boy
Angela	second place, poodle, Mama's Pride

 # Books and Barks

Set up a reading promotion to encourage students to read fiction and nonfiction about dogs (you could design a cat or mixed pet version if desired.) Have students read about dogs in such a way that they make tic-tac-toe. Hand out the worksheet from page 104 or 105. Have students record the date they finish each book and turn in the form by a date you designate. Books that are specifically mentioned follow. The others are main characters from a series by that author and students can read any book in the series.

- *Because of Winn-Dixie* by Kate DiCamillo. Candlewick Press, 2000. (3–5)
- *Chewy Louie* by Howie Schneider. Northland Publishing AZ, 2000. (K–2)
- *A Dog Called Kitty* by Bill Wallace. Holiday House, 1980. (3–5)
- *The Good Dog* by Avi. Simon & Schuster, 2001. (3–5)
- *Love That Dog* by Sharon Creech. HarperCollins, 2001. (3–5)
- *Ribsy* by Beverly Cleary. HarperCollins, 1992. (3–5)
- *Shiloh* by Phyllis Reynolds Naylor. Simon & Schuster, 1991. (3–5)
- *Sounder* by William Howard Armstrong. HarperCollins, 1976. (3–5)
- *The Stray Dog* by Marc Simont. HarperCollins, 2001. (K–2)
- *Strider* by Beverly Cleary. William Morrow & Co., 1991. (3–5)
- *Tornado* by Betsy Cromer Byars. HarperCollins, 1999. (3–5)

 # WebQuests

Pet Detective WebQuest
www.ri.net/schools/Central_Falls/ch/heazak/petdet.html
Have younger students do this WebQuest from Debbie Zakowski. Decisions must be made about the kind of pet that would be most helpful and desirable.

Betz's Pet Shop WebQuest
www.geocities.com/mrsevon/webquest.html
Older students will enjoy this WebQuest. Open a new Pet Shop with all six classes of animals.

 # Resources

General Dog Fiction Books:

Because of Winn-Dixie by Kate DiCamillo. Candlewick Press, 2000. (3–5)

Chewy Louie by Howie Schneider. Northland Publishing AZ, 2000. (K–2)

Dog Breath: The Horrible Trouble with Hally Tosis by Dav Pilkey. Blue Sky Press, 1994. (K–4)

A Dog Called Kitty by Bill Wallace. Holiday House, 1980. (3–5)

The Good Dog by Avi. Simon & Schuster, 2001. (3–5)

The Hallo-Weiner by Dav Pilkey. Blue Sky Press, 1995. (K–3)

Love That Dog by Sharon Creech. HarperCollins, 2001. (3–5)

My Life in Dog Years by Gary Paulsen. Bantam Doubleday Dell, 1998. (3–5)

Ribsy by Beverly Cleary. HarperCollins, 1992. (3–5)

Shiloh by Phyllis Reynolds Naylor. Simon & Schuster, 1991. (3–5)

Sounder by William Howard Armstrong. HarperCollins, 1976. (3–5)

The Stray Dog by Marc Simont. HarperCollins, 2001. (K–2)

Strider by Beverly Cleary. William Morrow & Co., 1991. (3–5)

Tornado by Betsy Cromer Byars. HarperCollins, 1999. (3–5)

Yo Aesop! Get a Load of These Fables by Paul Rosenthal. Simon & Schuster, 1998. (3–5)

Books About Working Dogs:

Animal Helpers for the Disabled by Deborah Kent. Scholastic Library Publishing, 2003. (3–5) Discusses guide dogs, service dogs and assistance dogs and what they do to help people with physical disabilities.

Canine Companions by Judith Presnall. Gale Group, 2003. (3–5) Presnall explains how service and companion dogs are chosen, trained and raised.

Detector Dogs: Sniffing Out Trouble by Alice McGinty. Rosen Publishing Group, 2003. (3–5) Various breeds can be trained to sniff out narcotics, people buried under snow or rubble and bombs.

Dogs Helping Kids with Feelings by Terry Vinocur. Rosen Publishing Group, 2003. (K–3) Dogs can be trained to help people deal with loneliness, anger, loss and psychological trauma.

Guide Dogs by Judith Presnall. Gale Group, 2001. (3–5) Contains information and photos to explain how dogs assist the vision-impaired.

Guide Dogs: From Puppies to Partners by Diana Lawrenson. Allen & Unwin, 2002. (4–5). This photo-journal shows the real stories of several dogs raised to assist their new owners.

Guide Dogs: Seeing for People Who Can't by Alice McGinty. Rosen Publishing Group, 2003. (K–3) This book follows Freedom, a puppy selected for the assistant dog program, from his puppy days to his pairing with his lucky new owner.

Helping Paws: Dogs that Serve by Melinda Luke. Scholastic, 2002. (K–3) This book for younger readers discusses why dogs and their senses are particularly qualified to assist the physically challenged and the police.

Police Dogs: Helping to Fight Crime by Alice McGinty. Rosen Publishing Group, 2003. (K–3) In following Jesse, students learn how dogs are selected, trained and used to help police fight crime and apprehend criminals.

Seaman: The Dog Who Explored the West with Lewis and Clark by Gail Karwoski. Peachtree Publishers, 2003. (3–5)

Shelter Dogs: Amazing Stories of Adopted Strays by Peg Kehret. Albert Whitman, 1999. (3–5)

Togo by Robert Blake. Philomel Books, 2002. (2–5) This is a fictionalized account of a 1925 diphtheria serum run from Anchorage to Nome, Alaska, led by Togo, a Siberian husky.

Working Like a Dog: The Story of Working Dogs Through History by Gena Gorrell. Tundra Books, 2003. (3–5) Students will meet a number of dogs and read about their work, including: Opal, a Labrador Retriever who guides a blind person; Servus, a dog that helped to search the World Trade Center ruins; a German Shepherd named Dart who searches for illegal seafood; and others.

Books About Selecting a Dog:

"Let's Get a Pup" Said Kate by Bob Graham. Candlewick Press, 2001. (K–2) A trip to the animal rescue center results in not one, but two perfect pets.

The Perfect Puppy for Me! by Jane O'Connor and Jessie Hartland. Viking, 2003. (K–2) Learn interesting facts in an entertaining narrative about lots of dogs, including the one that might be perfect for you. Interesting information tells readers that puppies lose their baby teeth, Newfoundland dogs have webbed feet and tomato juice will get the skunk stink off your dog. Includes a recipe for Harriet's Delicious Cookies for Dogs.

A Pup Just for Me; A Boy Just for Me by Dorothea Seeber. Philomel Books, 2000. (K–2) Compare the big step of pet adoption from the points of view of the child and the dog.

Books About Pets:

During Pet Month, display all your pet books. Here are some outstanding books about pet cats and dogs:

The American Shorthair Cat by Joanne Mattern. Capstone Press, 2002. (3–5) Part of the Learning About Cats series that includes 12 cat breeds. Every other page is a captioned full-color photograph. The book begins and ends with double-spreads of quick facts. Between them are chapters on the history and development of the breed and how to raise and care for it.

A Cat for You: Caring for Your Cat by Susan Blackaby. Picture Window Books, 2003. (K–3) Filled with interesting facts—a cat can fit through any opening the size of its head, most of the big cats can roar but cannot purr, the small cats can purr but cannot roar, etc. This book will be read and reread by readers of all ages. Also see *A Dog for You: Caring for Your Dog* by Susan Blackaby. Picture Window Books, 2003. (K–2)

Cats and ***Dogs*** by Helen Frost. Capstone Press, 2001. (K–1) With less than 45 words in each book, both books give basic facts with photos for very young readers.

Companion Dogs: More Than Best Friends by Elizabeth Ring. Millbrook Press, 1994. (K–2) Anecdotes and success stories tell how dogs have made the lives of their owners successful and more enjoyable.

Dog Poems by Myra Cohn Livingston. Holiday House, 1990. (K–5) Share these with your audiences to give them small, powerful and funny pictures of man's best friend.

Dogs by Gail Gibbons. Holiday House, 1996. (K–2) Simple text explains the history, breeds, habits and characteristics of a variety of dogs, including how to care for them.

The Greyhound by Charlotte Wilcox. Capstone Press, 2001. (3–5) Part of the Learning About Dogs series that includes 24 dog breeds. Packed with interesting facts about a variety of dogs. In this title, learn that few greyhounds are actually gray. If they are, the color is called blue.

How to Talk to Your Dog by Jean Craighead George. HarperCollins, 1999. (3–5) Learn ways to communicate with your pet so it knows you are the boss and that it has expectations and perks as your pet.

The Life Cycle of a Cat and *The Life Cycle of a Dog* by Lisa Trumbauer. Capstone Press, 2002. (K–1) The books show the life cycle of a tabby cat and a beagle in clear close-up photos and easy text. The glossary, index and resource list extend the learning.

Our Puppies Are Growing by Carolyn Otto. HarperCollins, 1998. (K–2) This is an easy-to-read explanation of the birth and growth of puppies through the eyes of their young owner. Extension activities for children and their parents end the book.

Web sites:

Betz's Pet Shop WebQuest
www.geocities.com/mrsevon/webquest.html

Dog Breath: The Horrible Trouble with Hally Tosis *Reader's Theater Script*
www.readinglady.com/Readers_Theater/Scripts/dogbreath.doc

Dogs in the Family
www.akc.org/life/family/index.cfm
Click on "Are You Ready for a Dog?," "The Right Dog for You" and even "Celebrating Holidays with Your Pet." The site includes an extensive checklist of how to make your dog's life the best it can be.

Doris: A Dog's Life *Reader's Theater Scrip*t
www.readinglady.com/Readers_Theater/Scripts/adogslife.doc

Guide Dogs for the Blind
www.guidedogs.com
Provides a wealth of information and photographs including how guide puppies are raised and trained and how one can volunteer. The site also offers an Educators Resource Guide with resource material, curriculum guides and classroom activity planners.

The Hallo-Wiener *Reader's Theater Script*
www.readinglady.com/Readers_Theater/Scripts/hallowiener.doc

Pet Detective WebQuest
www.ri.net/schools/Central_Falls/ch/heazak/petdet.html

Pet Finder
www.petfinder.org
Type in the type of pet you want and your location and see the animals available. This site will also tell you where your local shelters and rescue groups are and how to care for your pet. As I wrote this, there were more than 73,000 cats available and 87,000 dogs. There were also birds, horses, pigs, rabbits, reptiles and "small and furry" pets for adoption.

BINGO Illustrations

Calling All Pets!

Date: _____

Dear Parents,

In the library, we are learning about the many roles of dogs in the lives of humans. One important role is that of family companion. Your child is invited to bring in a photo of his or her pet cat, dog or other animal.

Photos should be no larger than 4" x 6". Attach the photo to a sheet of paper. Below the picture, please label the name of your pet and your child (see sample below):

Bonnie Miller's dog Sam

If you have more than one child, include all of their names. On the back of the paper, please write the name of your child's teacher to whom you want the photo returned.

Deadline for photos is _____.

Look for our display of beloved furry family members near the library. Pets will be on display until _____. After that, photos will be returned.

Thank you for your help and participation. If you have any questions, please call me at _____.

Sincerely,

Dog Show Logic Puzzle

Can you figure out what kind of dog each child owned and the place it received at the dog show? Place an "X" in each box that is incorrect. Place a star in the correct box. Write the dog's name in the last column. Once a star is determined, remember to "X" all of the boxes in the star's row and column.

Owner	1st Place	2nd Place	3rd Place	Poodle	Collie	Beagle	Dog's Name
Sarah							
Joey							
Angela							

Clues

1. Sarah's dog Tagalong is not a collie or poodle, but did come in first place.

2. Joey was disappointed when his Snappy Boy came in behind Mama's Pride.

3. The poodle beat Snappy Boy.

Name: _____   Teacher's Name: _____

Dogs, Dogs, Dogs!
Intermediate Version

In each box, write the date that you finished reading the book. For nonfiction books, write the author and title on the back of this form.

Your completed card is **due no later than** _____

Winn-Dixie DiCamillo	*Sounder* Armstrong	*Strider* Cleary	**Nonfiction**
Nonfiction	**Hank the Cowdog** Erickson	*A Dog Called Kitty* Wallace	*Shiloh* Naylor
Ribsy Cleary	*Tornado* Byars	**Nonfiction**	*Santa Paws* Edwards
Love That Dog Creech	**Nonfiction**	*The Good Dog* Avi	**Harold–Bunnicula** Howe

Italicized names are titles. If the name is not italicized, it is the dog's name in a series of books.

Name: _____   Teacher's Name: _____

Dogs, Dogs, Dogs!

Primary Version

In each box, write the date that you finished reading the book. For nonfiction books, write the author and title on the back of this form.

Your completed card is **due no later than** _____

Carl Day	***McDuff*** Wells	**Clifford** Bridwell	**Nonfiction**
Nonfiction	**Pinkerton** Kellogg	***The Stray Dog*** Simont	***Tiny*** Meister
Biscuit Capucilli	**Martha** Meddaugh	**Nonfiction**	**Mudge** Rylant
Kipper Inkpen	**Nonfiction**	***Chewy Louie*** Schneider	**Sally** Huneck

Italicized names are titles. If the name is not italicized, it is the dog's name in a series of books.

Bibliography

Books:

A

Abeyta, Jennifer. *Coins*. Scholastic Library Publishing, 2000.

Abeyta, Jennifer. *Stamps*. Scholastic Library Publishing, 2000.

Adamson, Heather. *A Day in the Life of a Farmer*. Capstone Press, 2004.

Alborough, Jez. *My Friend Bear*. Candlewick Press, 1998.

Appelt, Kathi. *Down Cut Shin Creek: The Pack Horse Librarians of Kentucky*. HarperCollins, 2001.

Arenson, Roberta. *One, Two, Skip a Few! First Number Rhymes*. Barefoot Books, 1998.

Armstrong, William Howard. *Sounder*. HarperCollins, 1976.

Armstrong-Ellis, Carey. *Prudy's Problem and How She Solved It*. Harry N. Abrams, 2002.

Artell, Mike. *Petite Rouge: A Cajun Red Riding Hood*. Dial, 2001.

Auch, Mary Jane. *The Princess and the Pizza*. Holiday House, 2002.

Avi. *The Good Dog*. Simon & Schuster, 2001.

Aylesworth, Jim. *Teddy Bear Tears*. Simon & Schuster, 1997.

B

Bailey, Linda. *Gordon Loggins and the Three Bears*. Kids Can Press, 1997.

Bang, Molly. *One Fall Day*. Greenwillow Books, 1994.

Bear, John. *The Frog and the Princess and the Prince and the Mole and the Frog and the Mole and the Princess ...* Ten Speed Press, 1994.

Best, Cari. *Red Light, Green Light, Mama and Me*. Orchard Books, 1995.

Beyer, Julie. *Miniature Cars*. Scholastic Library Publishing, 2000.

Birdseye, Tom. *Look Out, Jack! The Giant is Back!* Holiday House, 2001.

Blackaby, Susan. *A Cat for You: Caring for Your Cat*. Picture Window Books, 2003.

Blackaby, Susan. *A Dog for You: Caring for Your Dog*. Picture Window Books, 2003.

Blake, Robert. *Togo*. Philomel Books, 2002.

Blegvad, Lenore. *First Friends*. HarperCollins, 2000.

Blundell, Tony. *Beware of Boys*. Greenwillow Books, 1992.

Branley, Franklyn. *Snow is Falling*. HarperCollins, 2000.

Brett, Jan. *Goldilocks and the Three Bears*. Putnam, 1987.

Briggs, Raymond. *Jim and the Beanstalk*. Putnam, 1989.

Brown, Marc. *D. W.'s Library Card*. Little, Brown and Company, 2001.

Brown, Marc. *Locked in the Library!* Little, Brown and Company, 1998.

Bruss, Deborah. *Book! Book! Book!* Scholastic, 2000.

Buehner, Caralyn, and Mark. *Fanny's Dream*. Dial, 1996.

Bunting, Eve. *Anna's Table*. Northword Press, 2002.

Bunting, Eve. *A Picnic in October*. Harcourt, 1999.

Burke, Jennifer. *Cold Days*. Scholastic Library Publishing, 2000.

Burton, Jane, and Kim Taylor. *The Nature and Science of Autumn*. Gareth Stevens, 1999.

Burton, Jane, and Kim Taylor. *The Nature and Science of Rain*. Gareth Stevens, 1997.

Burton, Jane, and Kim Taylor. *The Nature and Science of Spring*. Gareth Stevens, 1999.

Burton, Jane, and Kim Taylor. *The Nature and Science of Winter*. Gareth Stevens, 1999.

Byars, Betsy Cromer. *Tornado*. HarperCollins, 1999

C

Calmenson, Stephanie. *The Principal's New Clothes*. Scholastic, 1991.

Carlson, Nancy. *Bunnies and Their Hobbies*. Lerner Publishing, 1984.

Carlstrom, Nancy White. *Jesse Bear, What Will You Wear?* Simon & Schuster, 1996.

Carr, Jan. *Splish, Splash, Spring*. Holiday House, 2001.

Christelow, Eileen. *Where's the Big Bad Wolf?* Clarion Books, 2002.

Cleary, Beverly. *Ribsy*. HarperCollins, 1992.

Cleary, Beverly. *Strider*. William Morrow & Co., 1991.

Clements, Andrew. *Double Trouble in Walla Walla*. Millbrook Press, 1997.

Cockrill, Pauline. *The Teddy Bear Encyclopedia*. DK Publishing, 2001.

Cole, Brock. *The Giant's Toe*. Farrar, Straus and Giroux, 1986.

Coleman, Janet Wyman. *Famous Bears and Friends: One Hundred Years of Stories, Poems, Songs, and Heroics*. Dutton, 2002.

Collins, Sheila Hebert. *'T Pousette et 't Poulette: A Cajun Hansel and Gretel*. Pelican Publishing Company, 2001.

Coutant, Helen. *First Snow*. Knopf, 1974.

Creech, Sharon. *Love That Dog*. HarperCollins, 2001.

Crummel, Susan Stevens. *Cook-a-Doodle-Doo*. Harcourt, 1999.

D

Dahl, Michael. Read-it! Joke Books series. Picture Window Books, 2003.

Davis, Aubrey. *Bone Button Borscht*. Kids Can Press, 1997.

Deedy, Carmen Agra. *The Library Dragon*. Peachtree Publishers, 1994.

DeGezelle, Terri. *Autumn*. Capstone Press, 2002.

DeGezelle, Terri. *Spring*. Capstone Press, 2002.

DeGezelle, Terri. *Winter*. Capstone Press, 2002.

Delessert, Etienne. *The Seven Dwarfs*. Creative Company, 2001.

DeLuise, Dom. *Dom DeLuise's Hansel and Gretel*. Simon & Schuster, 1997.

DiCamillo, Kate. *Because of Winn-Dixie*. Candlewick Press, 2000.

Dobkin, Bonnie. *Collecting*. Scholastic Library Publishing, 1993.

Doyle, Malachy. *Jody's Beans*. Candlewick Press, 1999.

E

Eclare, Melanie. *A Harvest of Color: Growing a Vegetable Garden*. Ragged Bears, 2001.

Ehlert, Lois. *Snowballs*. Harcourt, 1995.

Emberley, Rebecca. *Three Cool Kids*. Little, Brown and Company, 1995.

Enderlein, Cheryl L. Birthdays Around the World series. Capstone Press, 1998.

Engel, Diana. *Josephina, the Great Collector*. William Morrow & Co., 1988.

Ericsson, Jennifer A. *Out and About at the Bakery*. Picture Window Books, 2002. Part of the Field Trips series that also includes *Out and About at the Apple Orchard*, *Out and About at the Dairy Farm*, *Out and About at the Fire Station*, *Out and About at the Orchestra* and *Out and About at the Zoo*.

Erlbach, Aileen. *Happy Birthday Everywhere*. Millbrook Press, 1997.

Ernst, Lisa Campbell. *Goldilocks Returns*. Simon & Schuster, 2000.

Ernst, Lisa Campbell. *Little Red Riding Hood: A Newfangled Prairie Tale*. Simon & Schuster, 1995.

Ernst, Lisa Campbell. *Stella Louella's Runaway Book*. Simon & Schuster, 1998.

F

Fearnley, Jan. *Mr. Wolf and the Three Bears*. Harcourt, 2002.

Fearnley, Jan. *Mr. Wolf's Pancakes*. M E Media LLC, 2001.

Finnegan, Mary Pat. *Autumn: Signs of the Season Around North America*. Picture Window Books, 2002.

Finnegan, Mary Pat. *Winter: Signs of the Season Around North America*. Picture Window Books, 2002.

Flanagan, Alice. *Ms. Davison, Our Librarian*. Scholastic Library Publishing, 1996.

Fowler, Allan. *Corn—On and Off the Cob*. Scholastic Library Publishing, 1994.

Fowler, Allan. *It's a Fruit, It's a Vegetable, It's a Pumpkin*. Scholastic Library Publishing, 1995.

Fowler, Allan. *The Library of Congress*. Scholastic Library Publishing, 1996.

French, Fiona. *Snow White in New York*. Oxford University Press, 1990.

Freymann, Saxton, and Joost Elffers. *How Are You Peeling? Foods with Moods*. Scholastic, 1999.

Friedman, Debra. *Picture This: Fun Photography and Crafts*. Kids Can Press, 2003.

Friedman, Lise. *First Lessons in Ballet*. Workman Publishing, 1999.

Frost, Helen. *Cats*. Capstone Press, 2001.

Frost, Helen. *Dogs*. Capstone Press, 2001.

Frost, Helen. *Going to the Dentist*. Capstone Press, 1999.

G

Garcia, Jerry, and David Grisman. *The Teddy Bears' Picnic*. HarperCollins, 1999.

George, Jean Craighead. *How to Talk to Your Dog*. HarperCollins, 1999.

George, Lindsay. *In the Snow: Who's Been Here?* Greenwillow Books, 1995.

Gerard, Valerie J. *Spring: Signs of the Season Around North America*. Picture Window Books, 2002.

Gibbons, Gail. *Click! A Book About Cameras and Taking Pictures*. Little, Brown and Company, 1997.

Gibbons, Gail. *Dogs*. Holiday House, 1996.

Gibbons, Gail. *The Reasons for the Seasons*. Holiday House, 1995.

Gilbertsen, Neal. *Little Red Snapperhood: A Fishy Fairy Tale*. Graphic Arts Center Publishing Co., 2003.

Golenbock, Peter. *Teammates*. Harcourt, 1990.

Goode, Diane. *The Dinosaur's New Clothes: A Retelling of the Hans Christian Andersen Tale*. Blue Sky Press, 1999.

Gorrell, Gena. *Working Like a Dog: The Story of Working Dogs Through History*. Tundra Books, 2003.

Graham, Bob. *"Let's Get a Pup" Said Kate*. Candlewick Press, 2001.

Granger, Neill. *Stamp Collecting*. Millbrook Press, 1994.

Graves, Peter. *Greek Gods and Heroes*. Bantam Doubleday Dell, 1973.

Greenstein, Elaine. *As Big As You*. Random House, 2002.

Grey, Mini. *The Very Smart Pea and the Princess-to-Be*. Random House, 2003.

Guy, Ginger Foglesong. *¡Fiesta!* Greenwillow Books, 1996.

Gwynne, Fred. *Pondlarker*. Simon & Schuster, 1990.

H

Hall, Zoe. *Fall Leaves Fall!* Scholastic, 2000.

Harris, Jim. *Jack and the Giant: A Story Full of Beans*. Northland Publishing AZ, 1997.

Hartman, Bob. *The Wolf Who Cried Boy*. Putnam, 2002.

Hassett, John and Ann. *The Three Silly Girls Grubb*. Houghton Mifflin, 2002.

Henkes, Kevin. *Wemberly Worried*. Greenwillow Books, 2000.

Hooks, Kristine. *Dolls*. Scholastic Library Publishing, 2000.

Hopkins, Jackie Mims. *The Horned Toad Prince*. Peachtree Publishers, 2000.

Hopkins, Jackie Mims. *The Three Armadillies Tuff*. Peachtree Publishers, 2002.

Hoyt-Goldsmith, Diane. *Celebrating a Quinceañera: A Latina's Fifteenth Birthday Celebration*. Holiday House, 2002.

The Hutchinson Treasury of Teddy Bear Tales. Hutchinson, 1997.

J

Jackson, Bobby. *Little Red Ronnika*. Multicultural Publications, 1999.

January, Brendan, and the New York Public Library. *The New York Public Library Amazing Mythology: A Book of Answers for Kids*. John Wiley and Sons, 2000.

Jocelyn, Marthe. *Hannah's Collections*. Dutton, 2000.

Johnson, Sylvia. *How Leaves Change*. Lerner Publishing, 1986.

Johnston, Tony. *The Cowboy and the Black-eyed Pea*. Putnam, 1992.

K

Karwoski, Gail. *Seaman: The Dog Who Explored the West with Lewis and Clark*. Peachtree Publishers, 2003.

Katz, Alan. *I'm Still Here in the Bathtub: Brand New Silly Dilly Songs*. Simon & Schuster, 2003.

Katz, Alan. *Take Me Out of the Bathtub and Other Silly Dilly Songs*. Simon & Schuster, 2001.

Keats, Ezra Jack. *The Snowy Day*. Viking, 1998.

Kehret, Peg. *Shelter Dogs: Amazing Stories of Adopted Strays*. Albert Whitman, 1999.

Kellogg, Steven. *Jack and the Beanstalk.* William Morrow & Co., 1991.

Kent, Deborah. *Animal Helpers for the Disabled.* Scholastic Library Publishing, 2003.

Ketteman, Helen. *Bubba the Cowboy Prince: A Fractured Texas Tale.* Scholastic, 1997.

Ketteman, Helen. *Not Yet, Yvette.* Albert Whitman, 1992.

Kirkpatrick, Rob. *Trading Cards.* Scholastic Library Publishing, 2000.

Kleven, Elisa. *Hooray, A Piñata!* Dutton, 1996.

Klingel, Cynthia, and Robert B. Noyed. *School Librarians.* Rourke Press, 2001.

Klingel, Cynthia, and Robert B. Noyed. *Spring.* Child's World, 2000.

Kottke, Jan. *A Day with a Librarian.* Scholastic Library Publishing, 2000.

L

Laird, Donivee Martin. *The Three Little Hawaiian Pigs and the Magic Shark.* Barnaby Books, 1994.

Lakin, Patricia. *Clarence the Copy Cat.* Random House, 2002.

Landon, Lucinda. *Meg Mackintosh and the Mystery in the Locked Library: A Solve-it-Yourself Mystery.* Secret Passage Press, 1996.

Lankford, Mary. *Birthdays Around the World.* William Morrow & Co., 2000.

Lasky, Kathryn. *The Emperor's Old Clothes.* Harcourt, 1999.

Lasky, Kathryn. *Porkenstein.* Blue Sky Press, 2002.

Lawrenson, Diana. *Guide Dogs: From Puppies to Partners.* Allen & Unwin, 2002.

Lester, Helen. *Me First.* Houghton Mifflin, 1992.

Lester, Helen. *Tackylocks and the Three Bears.* Houghton Mifflin, 2002.

Lester, Helen. *Tacky the Penguin.* Houghton Mifflin, 1988.

Levine, Gail Carson. *Betsy Who Cried Wolf.* HarperCollins, 2002.

Levine, Gail Carson. *Ella Enchanted.* HarperCollins, 1997.

Lin, Grace. *The Ugly Vegetables.* Charlesbridge Publishing, 1999.

Lindenbaum, Pija. *Bridget and the Gray Wolves.* R & S Books, 2001.

Livingston, Myra Cohn. *Dog Poems.* Holiday House, 1990.

Lowell, Susan. *Dusty Locks and the Three Bears.* Henry Holt and Company, 2001.

Lowell, Susan. *Little Red Cowboy Hat.* Henry Holt and Company, 1997.

Lowell, Susan. *Three Little Javelinas.* Northland Publishing AZ, 1992.

Luke, Melinda. *Helping Paws: Dogs that Serve.* Scholastic, 2002.

M

Maccarone, Grace. *Three Pigs, One Wolf and Seven Magic Shapes.* Scholastic, 1997.

Mattern, Joanne. *The American Shorthair Cat.* Capstone Press, 2002.

McGinty, Alice. *Detector Dogs: Sniffing Out Trouble.* Rosen Publishing Group, 2003.

McGinty, Alice. *Guide Dogs: Seeing for People Who Can't.* Rosen Publishing Group, 2003.

McGinty, Alice. *Police Dogs: Helping to Fight Crime.* Rosen Publishing Group, 2003.

McKissack, Patricia. *Goin' Someplace Special.* Simon & Schuster, 2001.

Meddaugh, Susan. *Cinderella's Rat.* Houghton Mifflin, 1997.

Meister, Cari. *Tiny Goes to the Library.* Viking, 2000.

Meyers, Cindy. *Rolling Along with Goldilocks and the Three Bears.* Woodbine House, 1999.

Miller, Pat. *Stretchy Library Lessons: Reading Activities.* UpstartBooks, 2003.

Miller, William. *Richard Wright and the Library Card.* Lee & Low Books, 1997.

Minters, Frances. *Cinder-Elly.* Viking, 1994.

Mitchell, Marianne. *Joe Cinders.* Henry Holt and Company, 2002.

Moerbeek, Kees. *The Diary of Hansel and Gretel.* Simon & Schuster, 2002.

Mora, Pat. *Tomás and the Library Lady.* Random House, 1997.

Morris, Ann. *How Teddy Bears Are Made: A Visit to the Vermont Teddy Bear Factory.* Scholastic, 1994.

Munro, Roxie, and Julie Cummins. *The Inside-Outside Book of Libraries.* Dutton, 1996.

Munsch, Robert. *Moira's Birthday.* Annick Press, 1988.

Murphy, Frank. *The Legend of the Teddy Bear.* Sleeping Bear Press, 2000.

N

Naylor, Phyllis Reynolds. *Shiloh.* Simon & Schuster, 1991.

Newell, Patrick. *Military Collectibles.* Scholastic Library Publishing, 2000.

Nicholas, Christopher. *Know-It-Alls: Bears!* Learning Horizons, Inc., 2000.

O

O'Connor, Jane, and Jessie Hartland. *The Perfect Puppy for Me!* Viking, 2003.

Osborne, Mary Pope. *Kate and the Beanstalk.* Simon & Schuster, 2000.

Otto, Carolyn. *Our Puppies Are Growing.* HarperCollins, 1998.

Owens, Thomas S. *Collecting Baseball Cards.* Millbrook Press, 2000.

Owens, Thomas S. *Collecting Basketball Cards.* Millbrook Press, 1998.

P

Parks, Carmen. *Farmers Market.* Harcourt, 2003.

Paulsen, Gary. *Hatchet.* Atheneum, 1987.

Paulsen, Gary. *My Life in Dog Years.* Bantam Doubleday Dell, 1998.

Pearson, Mary E. *I Can Do It All.* Scholastic Library Publishing, 2002.

Pilkey, Dav. *Dog Breath: The Horrible Trouble with Hally Tosis.* Blue Sky Press, 1994.

Pilkey, Dav. *The Hallo-Weiner.* Blue Sky Press, 1995.

Posner, Pat. *Gods and Goddesses from Greek Myths.* McGraw-Hill Children's Publishing, 2003.

Presnall, Judith. *Canine Companions.* Gale Group, 2003.

Presnall, Judith. *Guide Dogs.* Gale Group, 2001.

R

Radabaugh, Melinda. *Going to the Library.* Heinemann Library, 2002.

Ransford, Sandy. *First Riding Lessons.* Houghton Mifflin, 2002.

Ready, Dee. *Librarians.* Capstone Press, 1998.

Richardson, Adele D. and Lola M. Schaefer. *Bears: Paws, Claws, and Jaws.* Capstone Press, 2001.

Ring, Elizabeth. *Companion Dogs: More Than Best Friends.* Millbrook Press, 1994.

Robbins, Ken. *Autumn Leaves.* Scholastic, 1998.

Rockwell, Anne. *One Bean.* Walker and Company, 1998.

Roop, Connie, and Peter. *A Teddy Bear for President Roosevelt.* Scholastic, 2002.

Rosales, Melodye Benson. *Leola and the Honeybears: An African-American Retelling of Goldilocks and the Three Bears.* Scholastic, 1999.

Rosen, Michael. *We're Going on a Bear Hunt.* Simon & Schuster, 1989.

Rosenthal, Paul. *Yo Aesop! Get a Load of These Fables.* Simon & Schuster, 1998.

Ross, Tony. *Goldilocks & the Three Bears.* Overlook, 1992.

Ross, Tony. *Stone Soup.* Puffin, 1991.

Rylant, Cynthia. *In November.* Harcourt, 2000.

Rylant, Cynthia. *Poppleton in Winter.* Blue Sky Press, 2001.

S

Sachar, Louis. *Sideways Stories From Wayside School.* William Morrow & Co., 1998.

San Souci, Robert D. *Cinderella Skeleton.* Harcourt, 2000.

Saunders-Smith, Gail. *Animals in the Fall.* Capstone Press, 1997.

Saunders-Smith, Gail. *Autumn Leaves.* Capstone Press, 1998.

Saunders-Smith, Gail. *Fall Harvest.* Capstone Press, 1998.

Saunders-Smith, Gail. *Spring.* Capstone Press, 1998.

Saunders-Smith, Gail. *Warm Clothes*. Capstone Press, 1997.

Saunders-Smith, Gail. *Winter*. Capstone Press, 1998.

Schaefer, Lola M. *A Cold Day*. Capstone Press, 1999.

Schaefer, Lola M. *A Rainy Day*. Capstone Press, 1999.

Schaefer, Lola M. *A Snowy Day*. Capstone Press, 1999.

Schaefer, Lola M. *We Need Farmers*. Capstone Press, 1999.

Schaefer, Lola M. *A Windy Day*. Capstone Press, 1999.

Schneider, Howie. *Chewy Louie*. Northland Publishing AZ, 2000.

Schnur, Steven. *Autumn: An Alphabet Acrostic*. Clarion Books, 1997.

Schnur, Steven. *Spring: An Alphabet Acrostic*. Clarion Books, 1999.

Schnur, Steven. *Winter: An Alphabet Acrostic*. Clarion Books, 2002.

Schuette, Sarah L. *An Alphabet Salad: Fruits and Vegetables from A to Z*. Capstone Press, 2003.

Schuette, Sarah L. *Eating Pairs: Counting Fruits and Vegetables by Twos*. Capstone Press, 2003.

Scieszka, Jon. *The Frog Prince—Continued*. Viking, 1991.

Scieszka, Jon. *The True Story of the 3 Little Pigs*. Viking, 1989.

Seeber, Dorothea. *A Pup Just for Me; A Boy Just for Me*. Philomel Books, 2000.

Shetterly, Susan Hand. *Muwin and the Magic Hare*. Simon & Schuster, 1993.

Simon, Charnan. *Andrew Carnegie: Builder of Libraries*. Scholastic Library Publishing, 1997.

Simont, Marc. *The Stray Dog*. HarperCollins, 2001.

Smith, Cynthia Leitich. *Jingle Dancer*. William Morrow & Co., 2000.

Souhami, Jessica. *No Dinner! The Story of the Old Woman and the Pumpkin*. Marshall Cavendish, 2000.

Speed, Toby. *Brave Potatoes*. Putnam, 2000.

Spohn, David. *Winter Wood*. HarperCollins, 1991.

Stadler, Alexander. *Beverly Billingsly Borrows a Book*. Harcourt, 2002.

Stanley, Diane. *Goldie and the Three Bears*. HarperCollins, 2003.

Steig, William. *Sylvester and the Magic Pebble*. Simon & Schuster, 1988.

Stevens, Janet. *Tops & Bottoms*. Harcourt, 1995.

Stille, Darlene. *Fall*. Compass Point Books, 2001.

Stille, Darlene. *Spring*. Compass Point Books, 2001.

Stille, Darlene. *Winter*. Compass Point Books, 2001.

Sturges, Philemon. *The Little Red Hen Makes a Pizza*. Dutton, 1999.

T

Thaler, Mike. *The Librarian from the Black Lagoon*. Scholastic, 1997.

Trivizas, Eugene. *The Three Little Wolves and the Big Bad Pig*. Simon & Schuster, 1993.

Trumbauer, Lisa. *The Life Cycle of a Cat*. Capstone Press, 2002.

Trumbauer, Lisa. *The Life Cycle of a Dog*. Capstone Press, 2002.

Trumbauer, Lisa. *Seasons*. Capstone Press, 2000.

Turkle, Brinton. *Deep in the Forest*. Puffin, 1992.

V

Van Genechten, Guido. *Potty Time*. Simon & Schuster, 2001.

Vinocur, Terry. *Dogs Helping Kids with Feelings*. Rosen Publishing Group, 2003.

W

Waldherr, Kris. *Persephone and the Pomegranate: A Myth from Greece*. Penguin Putnam, 1993.

Wallace, Bill. *A Dog Called Kitty*. Holiday House, 1980.

Wallace, John. *Tiny Rabbit Goes to a Birthday Party*. Holiday House, 2000.

Warner, Gertrude Chandler. *The Deserted Library Mystery*. Albert Whitman, 1991.

Wells, Rosemary. *Yoko's Paper Cranes*. Hyperion, 2001.

Whatley, Bruce. *Wait! No Paint!* HarperCollins, 2001.

Wilcox, Charlotte. *The Greyhound*. Capstone Press, 2001.

Williams, Suzanne. *Library Lil*. Dial, 1997.

Willis, Jeanne. *The Boy Who Thought He Was a Teddy Bear: A Fairy Tale.* Peachtree Publishers, 2002.

Wilson, Karma. *Bear Snores On.* Simon & Schuster, 2001.

Wolff, Patricia R. *The Toll-Bridge Troll.* Harcourt, 1995.

Y

Yerxa, Leo. *Last Leaf First Snowflake to Fall.* Orchard Books, 1994.

Yolen, Jane. *No Bath Tonight.* HarperCollins, 1978.

Z

Zalben, Jane Breskin. *Don't Go.* Clarion Books, 2001.

Web sites:

Animal Tracks
www.leslietryon.com/animals1101/animalfootprints.html

Autumn Leaves
www.brainpop.com/science/ecology/autumnleaves/index.weml?&tried_cookie=true

BabyAnt.com
www.babyant.com/bt037114.html

Barbie® Collecting Start Page
www.collectdolls.about.com/library/blmcnu2.htm?PM=ss16_collectdolls#Gen

The Bear Den—Species by Species
www.bearden.org/species.html

Betz's Pet Shop
www.geocities.com/mrsevon/webquest.html

Carnegie for Kids
www.carnegie.org/sub/kids/libraries.html

Cartoon Classroom: Brick by Brick
Library.thinkquest.org/3538

CoinMasters.org
www.coinmasters.org

Common Fall Leaves
www.conservation.state.mo.us/nathis/seasons/fall/fleaves/fleaves.htm

Dog Breath: The Horrible Trouble with Hally Tosis *Reader's Theater Script*
www.readinglady.com/Readers_Theater/Scripts/dogbreath.doc

Dogs in the Family
www.akc.org/life/family/index.cfm

Dole 5 A Day Fruits and Vegetables
www.dole5aday.com/Kids/K_Index.jsp

Doris: A Dog's Life *Reader's Theater Script*
www.readinglady.com/Readers_Theater/Scripts/adogslife.doc

Double Trouble in Walla Walla *Reader's Theater Script*
www.readinglady.com/Readers_Theater/Scripts/doubletrouble.doc

Fall Crafts
www.enchantedlearning.com/crafts/fall

Fall Fever
www.funschool.com/php/games/game.php?g=arcade_ld2_ds1

Fall Online Games
www.kidsdomain.com/games/fall.html

First Lines
scils.rutgers.edu/%7Ekvander/firstlinesindex.html

Go Exploring in Books *Reader's Theater Script*
www.lisablau.com/scripts/2001scripts/GoExploringinBooks.doc

Guide Dogs for the Blind
www.guidedogs.com

The Hallo-Wiener *Reader's Theater Script*
www.readinglady.com/Readers_Theater/Scripts/hallowiener.doc

Hangman
superkids.com/aweb/tools/words/hangman

IPL Kidspace
ipl.sils.umich.edu/div/kidspace

JigZone
www.jigzone.com

The Jokester
www.thejokester.net

Junior Philatelists of America
www.jpastamps.org

Kids Ag Page
www.agr.state.il.us/kidspage/index.html

Kids' Place Games
eduplace.com/kids/games.html

KidStamps
www.kidstamps.com

Kids Web: The Digital Library for K–12 Students
www.npac.syr.edu/textbook/kidsweb

Leaf Invaders
www.conservation.state.mo.us/nathis/seasons/fall/swl
eaf/swleaf.htm

Mancala
imagiware.com/mancala

Me First *Reader's Theater Script*
www.readinglady.com/Readers_Theater/Scripts/me
first.doc

Moira's Birthday *Reader's Theater Script*
www.qesn.meq.gouv.qc.ca/schools/bchs/rtheatre/
sample.htm

The Mystery Master Logic Puzzles
www.mysterymaster.com/puzzles/WinterBreaks.html

The New Improved Fruit Game
www.2020tech.com/fruit/index.html

No Bath Tonight *Reader's Theater Script*
hometown.aol.com/rcswallow/NoBathTonight.html

Pet Detective WebQuest
www.ri.net/schools/Central_Falls/ch/heazak/petdet.
html

Pet Finder
www.petfinder.org

Room 108 Games
www.scugog-net.com/room108/starflight/games1.html

Science U: Seasons Reasons
www.scienceu.com/observatory/articles/seasons/
seasons.html

Snowballs *Reader's Theater Script*
www.readinglady.com/Readers_Theater/Scripts/Snow
balls.doc

Spring Crafts
www.enchantedlearning.com/crafts/spring

Spring Online Games
www.kidsdomain.com/games/spring.html

Story of Persephone
www.windows.ucar.edu/tour/link=/mythology/perse
phone_seasons.html&edu=high

The Story of the Teddy Bear
www.theodoreroosevelt.org/kidscorner/tr_teddy.htm

Tacky the Penguin *Reader's Theater Script*
www.readinglady.com/Readers_Theater/Scripts/Tacky
_the_Penguin.doc

Teddy Bear Story—100 Years of the Teddy Bear
www.liverpoolmuseum.org.uk/teddies

10 Reasons a Dog Shouldn't Use a Computer
merel.us/Joker/AnimalFrame.htm

10,000 Year Calendar
www.calendarhome.com/tyc

Three Sideways Stories from Wayside School *Reader's Theater Script*
www.aaronshep.com/rt/RTE32.html

Upstart
www.highsmith.com

Wemberly Worried *Reader's Theater Script*
www.readinglady.com/Readers_Theater/Scripts/
wemberly.doc

What Grows?
www.kidsfarm.com/crops.htm

Winter Celebrations: WebQuest for Second Grade
jets.utep.edu/helen_ball/awauson/winter/adria
wauson/index.htm

Winter Crafts
www.enchantedlearning.com/crafts/winter

Winter Fun Links to Learning
www.mikids.com/winterfun.html

Winter Online Games
www.kidsdomain.com/games/winter.html

The Winter Solstice
www.mikids.com/december.html

Word Central's Student Dictionary
www.wordcentral.com

Zoom Party
pbskids.org/zoom/party